821
L282p
M984p

D0793403

821   Murtaugh
L282p   Piers Plowman and the
M984p   image of God

CHRISTIAN HERITAGE COLLEGE
2100 Greenfield Dr.
El Cajon, CA 92021

Piers Plowman
and
the Image of God

DANIEL MAHER MURTAUGH

A University of Florida Book

The University Presses of Florida
Gainesville / 1978

Library of Congress Cataloging in Publication Data

Murtaugh, Daniel Maher.
  Piers Plowman and the image of God.

  Originally presented as the author's thesis,
Yale.
  "A University of Florida book."
  Includes bibliographical references and index.
  1. Langland, William, 1330?–1400? Piers the
Plowman. 2. Image of God in literature. I. Title.
PR2017.I4M8 1978   821′.1   77–25544
ISBN 0–8130–0534–5

The University Presses of Florida is the
scholarly publishing agency for the
State University System of Florida.

COPYRIGHT © 1978 BY THE BOARD OF
REGENTS OF THE STATE OF FLORIDA

TYPOGRAPHY BY MODERN TYPOGRAPHERS, INCORPORATED
CLEARWATER, FLORIDA

PRINTED BY STORTER PRINTING CO., INCORPORATED
GAINESVILLE, FLORIDA

Acknowledgments

THIS STUDY had its remote origins in a Middle English seminar at Holy Cross College conducted by Thomas J. Grace, S.J., an inspiring teacher who raised many of the questions about *Piers Plowman* that I have since tried to answer. To my sorrow, I can now only guess at his judgment of my work and give him thanks in a memorial dedication for his share in its best pages.

My work first took clear shape as a doctoral dissertation written at Yale University under the direction of E. Talbot Donaldson, and it had at every stage the benefit of his penetrating and constructive criticism and his unsurpassed knowledge of the manuscript tradition.

Marie Borroff, Douglas Cole, and Alice Miskimin also read the original manuscript and made many helpful suggestions for its improvement. R. H. Bowers and Thomas D. Hill read and criticized later versions with clear-eyed sympathy. Valuable information and counsel also came from George Kane and Robert Levine. I am grateful to the Danforth Foundation for the graduate fellowship that supported me as I wrote the original dissertation, and to the Graduate School of Boston University for its help in defraying typing expenses at a later stage.

Finally, I should like to thank my dear wife, Kristen, for her good humor and moral support through the last several years of my tenancy on Piers's half-acre.

39306

*To my mother and father
and to the memory of
Thomas J. Grace, S.J.*

Contents

1. The Image of God   1

2. The Dialectic of Truth   5

3. The Social Dimension   31

4. Learning and Grace   63

5. The Pardon, Piers, and Christ   98

6. The Essential Poem at
     the Centre of Things   123

Index   127

1. The Image of God

A COMMON EXPERIENCE of those coming to *Piers Plowman* for the first time is a sense of surprise that, somehow or other, the whole thing does manage to hold together. It can easily be said—and it often is—that here and here Langland has lost control of his materials, but one cannot escape the general impression that he has a good deal more control over them than we do. The materials are certainly vast and varied. In the words of one critic they are "nothing less than the history of Christianity as it unfolds both in the world of the Old and New Testaments and in the heart of the individual Christian— two seemingly distinct realms between which the poet's allegory moves with dizzying rapidity."[1] It is this movement that I shall attempt to chart, since it is the chief problem and the chief glory of the poem. Movement implies life, and in the present study I should like to examine *Piers Plowman* in the light of certain pervasive elements of medieval thought which had a potential for the sort of life Langland's voice would give them.

Studies of Langland's intellectual backgrounds have advanced beyond attempts to align *Piers Plowman* closely with medieval schemata of scriptural exegesis or spiritual life. The fourfold sense of scripture and the "Three Lives" of Walter Hilton and others certainly show tendencies of thought that are reflected in Langland's poem, but

---

1. E. Talbot Donaldson, in *The Norton Anthology of English Literature, Revised*, ed. M. H. Abrams, Donaldson, et al. (New York: W. W. Norton and Co., 1968), 1:274.

their direct and univocal application has been found reductive.[2] Some
more recent students of Langland's intellectual debts have allowed
him a good deal more freedom but have still tended to trim his work
to fit its sources. Thus one critic tells us that *Piers Plowman* is "apocalyptic," that its emphasis is social and historical rather than individual and subjective.[3] Another tells us that it is mystical, that it
follows in the intense subjective tradition of Saint Bernard, that its
emphasis is almost exclusively individual and only metaphorically
social and historical.[4] The trouble with each approach is not in what
it affirms but in what it denies. In Langland we have a poet who,
when faced with two alternative modes of meaning, generally tries for
both at once.

A trend of medieval thought which seems conducive to this sort of
synthetic procedure takes as its point of departure the commonplace
notion suggested in my title: that man was created in the image and
likeness of God. This idea was appealed to explicitly or implicitly by
all medieval thinkers, in connection with an astonishing range of
topics. Augustine found images of the Trinity in human self-consciousness and in memory, intellect, and will. Saint Bernard developed
the idea mystically, saying that man bore God's image indelibly and
that he restored the divine likeness, lost by sin, as he approached
contemplation. On the other side of the ill-guarded border between
theology and philosophy, many thinkers tended to explain epistemology by a comparison with the procession of the Trinity or with the
divine act of Creation. The same thinkers might also explain the

2. The most consistent attempt to apply the methods of scriptural exegesis
to the poem is in D. W. Robertson and Bernard F. Huppé, *Piers Plowman and
Scriptural Tradition* (Princeton: Princeton University Press, 1951). See criti-
cisms by Morton W. Bloomfield in *Speculum* 27 (1952):245–49, and *Modern
Philology* 56 (1956):73–78; and by Donaldson in Dorothy Bethurum, ed.,
Critical Approaches to Medieval Literature (New York: Columbia University
Press, 1960), pp. 1–26. The "Three Lives" interpretation was first proposed by
Henry W. Wells, "The Construction of Piers Plowman," *PMLA* 44 (1929):
123–49; and adopted by R. W. Chambers, *Man's Unconquerable Mind* (London: Jonathan Cape, 1939), pp. 102–3; and by Nevill Coghill, "The Character
of Piers Plowman Considered from the B-Text," *Medium Aevum* 2 (1933):
108–35. See criticisms by R. W. Frank, *Piers Plowman and the Scheme of Salvation* (New Haven: Yale University Press, 1957), pp. 34–44.

3. Morton W. Bloomfield, *Piers Plowman as a Fourteenth-Century Apocalypse* (New Brunswick, N.J.: Rutgers University Press, n.d. [1962]), pp. 99,
105, and passim.

4. Edward Vasta, *The Spiritual Basis of Piers Plowman* (The Hague: Mouton, 1965), pp. 33–37, and passim.

Trinity or the Creation by comparisons with epistemology. The argument could change directions without warning, and so the relation of divine and human was not finally logical but metaphorical. Furthermore, if the divine Mind gave concrete expression to Its ideas in the order of the visible universe, it could follow that Its image, the human mind, could give a similarly concrete expression of its ideas in that part of creation which was its most direct responsibility: the order of society. As society approached a perfect image of man's rational nature, it could be said to reveal in a corporate way the Exemplar of that nature, the divine Mind Itself. It seems to me that this elaboration of the idea of man as the image of God constitutes a chief poetic resource in medieval thought, and that Langland recognized it as such.

The tradition certainly seems to shed light on the bewildering structure of Langland's poem, with its constant changes of setting and perspective and its insistence on real and immediate connections between areas of experience which, to the modern reader, seem completely disconnected. The action of the poem takes place at once in society and within the dreamer-narrator. Its time is at once the fourteenth-century present and various crucial moments in sacred history, most recurrently the moment of the Redemption. It speaks of the relation of man to his Creator and of the proper management of a money economy in the same terms, as if, indeed, the two subjects were the same seen under two aspects. These strategies of the poem suggest a view of reality as total metaphor, seen most clearly as such when the human mind looks through it to reality's source and its own exemplar in the divine Mind.

Man's status as the image and likeness of God is given its most poignant expression in the Incarnation. Here, in Christ's assumption of humanity and His performance of human good works, man's nature and works gain a value they do not have of themselves. Hence, simply to "Do-well" has consequences that reach into the realm of mystery. The dreamer of *Piers Plowman* searches for the meaning of "Do-well" and eventually finds it not in a discursive formulation but in the all-sufficient Person of Christ, Whose Redemption is achieved through the human nature the dreamer first knew as Piers. The many moral issues raised in the poem converge on this figure, who thus unifies the poem despite his infrequent appearances in it.

In attempting to describe how all these things happen, I shall deal primarily with the B-text. On several occasions, though, I shall consider passages added or given new developments in the C-text. Often the consistency of certain revisions in C can confirm the existence of an important motif in B and cast some new light on the general literary relations of the two versions. I am assuming throughout that the A-, B-, and C-texts are substantially the work of one author, William Langland. The textual and circumstantial evidence for such an assumption has recently been set forth by George Kane,[5] and I can add to his persuasive arguments the fact that unity of authorship works very well as an hypothesis for literary criticism.

5. *Piers Plowman: The Evidence for Authorship* (London: University of London, Athlone Press, 1965).

2. The Dialectic of Truth

LANGLAND'S THOUGHT moves most rapidly in some of his more theoretical and psychological passages, and I begin with a consideration
of four of these: the speech of Lady Holy Church, Piers's directions
for finding Truth, Wit's account of the "Castle of *Caro*," and the Tree
of Charity "amyddes mannes body."

Most readers of *Piers Plowman* have recognized the importance of
Lady Holy Church's speech in laying the doctrinal groundwork for
the whole poem. It also introduces one of the key poetic methods
which will recur throughout, for in *Piers Plowman* doctrine and poetic
method are curiously intertwined. Lady Holy Church uses the word
"truth" in a remarkable way. She descends from the "toure on a toft"
to the Field of Folk and uses the word as a name for God, perhaps
God the Father, with a clear emphasis on His transcendence:

> "The tour on þe toft," quod she, "truþe is þerInne,
> And wolde þat ye wrouȝte as his word techeþ.
> For he is fader of feiþ, and formed yow alle
> Boþe with fel and with face, and yaf yow fyue wittes
> For to worshipe hym þerwiþ while ye ben here."
>
> (B.I.12–16)[1]

1. I cite the following editions of *Piers Plowman* throughout: George Kane,
ed., *Piers Plowman: The A Version* (London: University of London, Athlone
Press, 1960); George Kane and E. Talbot Donaldson, eds., *Piers Plowman:
The B Version* (London: University of London, Athlone Press, 1975); and
(for the C-text, except where noted) Walter W. Skeat, ed., *The Vision of*

Some fifty lines later, after Lady Holy Church has identified herself, the dreamer, on his knees, asks her how he may save his soul. She responds with a different use of the term:

> "Whan alle tresors arn tried treuþe is þe beste;
> I do it on *Deus caritas* to deme þe soþe.
> It is as dereworþe a drury as deere god hymseluen.
> For who is trewe of his tonge, telleþ noon ooþer,
> Dooþ þe werkes þerwiþ and wilneþ no man ille,
> He is a god by þe gospel, a grounde and o lofte,
> And ek ylik to oure lord by Seint Lukes wordes."
>
> (B.I.85–91)[2]

We should pause over these lines because they involve the sort of complication that the whole poem will develop. "Truth" now does not seem to mean "God" but something else as valuable "as deere god hymseluen." It is no longer transcendent, but is in each man who "is trewe of his tonge" and lives a moral life. But the term cannot be transferred to the immanent without bringing some of its transcendent character with it, so that the "trewe" man becomes "a god by þe gospel a grounde and o lofte." His good works resound in heaven because they are the expression of Truth, at once the principle of moral action and heaven's King.

It is tempting to see in these last two lines the mystical doctrine of "deification," according to which the soul in contemplation restores its "likeness" (*similitudo*) to God to its full clarity and achieves a transitory foretaste of the Beatific Vision.[3] But I think we must resist this temptation because Lady Holy Church makes no specific reference

---

William Concerning Piers the Plowman, In Three Parallel Texts . . . , 2 vols. (London: Oxford University Press, 1886), hereafter *Parallel Texts*. I have eliminated the raised period with which Skeat separates half-lines and have silently supplied the punctuation that this sometimes obviates. I have also omitted editorial apparatus in quoting Kane and Donaldson.

2. The text in Luke is uncertain. Skeat suggests Luke 16:10–13 or 8:21 (see *Parallel Texts*, 2:23). T. P. Dunning, *Piers Plowman: An Interpretation of the A-Text* (Dublin: Talbot Press, 1937), p. 44, suggests Luke 6:35. Any of these, and many more, would fit here.

3. As does Edward Vasta, *Spiritual Basis*, pp. 68–83, taking up a suggestion made somewhat tentatively and in another connection by Greta Hort, *Piers Plowman and Contemporary Religious Thought* (London: Macmillan, n.d. [1937]), pp. 81, 115, and Donaldson, *Piers Plowman: The C-Text and Its Poet* (New Haven: Yale University Press, 1949), p. 186.

to the disciplines of mysticism. She refers instead to the ordinary life of good works. Still, by her account, this ordinary goodness has repercussions which do seem to suggest something as extraordinary as mystical contemplation. What she seems to be doing is instructing the dreamer in the total meaning of ethical actions in a universe informed by grace. The lesson is as difficult to grasp in discursive terms as is the ambiguity of that central term "truth." Morality is readily intelligible on a strictly natural plane, but if one introduces its supernatural dimension, it becomes a mystery.

The argument has gotten beyond Will the dreamer. What exactly does she mean by "truth"? " 'Yet haue I no kynde knowyng,' quod I, 'ye mote kenne me bettre, / By what craft in my cors it comseþ, and where' " (B.I.138–39). Her answer to this "doted daffe" is, if anything, more difficult than what went before:

> "It is a kynde knowyng, þat kenneþ in þyn herte
> For to louen þi lord leuere þan þiselue.
> No dedly synne to do, deye þeiʒ þow sholdest,
> This I trowe be truþe; who kan teche þee bettre,
> Loke þow suffre hym to seye and siþen lere it after.
> For þus witnesseþ his word; werche þow þerafter.
> For truþe telleþ þat loue is triacle of heuene:
> May no synne be on hym seene þat vseþ þat spice,
> And alle hise werkes he wrouʒte with loue as hym liste;
> And lered it Moyses for þe leueste þyng and moost lik to heuene,
> And ek þe plante of pees, moost precious of vertues.
> For heuene myʒte nat holden it, so heuy it semed,
> Til it hadde of þe erþe yeten hitselue.[4]
> And whan it hadde of þis fold flessh and blood taken
> Was neuere leef vpon lynde lighter þerafter,
> And portatif and persaunt as þe point of a nedle
> That myʒte noon Armure it lette ne none heiʒe walles.
>
> . . . .
>
> And for to knowen it kyndely, it comseþ by myght,
> And in þe herte þere is þe heed and þe heiʒe welle.
> For in kynde knowynge in herte þer comseþ a myʒt,
> And þat falleþ to þe fader þat formed vs alle,

4. The phrase means "alloyed itself" and stands for Skeat's "yeten his fylle" ("eaten his fill," which involves a doubtful past participle form, but which reflects the widely attested reading "eten his fille").

Loked on vs wiþ loue and leet his sone dye
Mekely for oure mysdedes to amenden vs alle."

                                                    (B.I.143–58, 163–68)

Here we have one of those explosions of meaning that make Langland
so fascinating and difficult a writer. If we follow the rapid movement
of his thought with care, we shall find that he starts out from and returns to the idea of truth as a natural knowledge of morality. By it
we are taught to love God and dread sin (143–45) and to know the
moral law by which our misdeeds are judged (cf. 161–62). But we
are also given a larger view which transforms the commonplace into
mystery. Somehow our knowledge of the moral law implies the central events of redemptive history. Truth, used here in both the transcendent and immanent senses, teaches us the moral law which is
basically a law of love, as Jesus told the scribes (Mark 12:29–31).
But returning to the text *Deus caritas*, we see that love is God and
hence is truth. The consciousness of God as love inevitably implies
the Incarnation, which Langland depicts in a burst of philosophic
and scriptural imagery.[5] When we are told that "alle [God's or
Truth's] werkes he wrouзte with loue as hym liste," we recall the
Second Person of the Trinity, the Word of God through Whom all
things were made (John 1:3). God was so heavy with this "triacle of
heuene" that it, or He, fell to the earth and took earth unto Himself
(or alloyed Himself with it, in Langland's striking image). In the
midst of this the moral law is introduced once again in such a way as
to stress Truth's transcendent aspect. Truth taught this to Moses, that
love is the dearest thing and most like to heaven. Here, as later in the
poem (B.XVII.1–16), the Old Testament episode that should be
uppermost in our mind is the most obvious one, the giving of the Ten
Commandments.

So the concept of truth is given a new complication. Not only is it
transcendent and immanent, God Himself and the inner principle of
man's moral actions; it is also cognitive and affective at the same
time. Natural knowledge, "kynde knowyng," actually implies love.
Furthermore, the process by which the truth we know in our hearts

5. See P. M. Kean, "Langland and the Incarnation," *Review of English
Studies* 16 (1965): 349–63, for an account of the scriptural and philosophical
backgrounds of these lines. Another such account is in Ben H. Smith, Jr.,
Traditional Imagery of Charity in Piers Plowman (The Hague: Mouton, 1966),
pp. 21–40, marred slightly by a misreading of the syntax of lines 148–49 (p.
24).

emerges in the world as good works actually seems to reproduce the process by which heaven's Truth, heavy with Love, descended to alloy itself with earth. This is the hard lesson of Lady Holy Church. The dreamer's failure fully to grasp the link of knowing to loving and of both to the Incarnate Christ eventually leads to his anti-intellectualism in Passus XI.

A subsequent passage, Piers's directions for finding Truth, builds directly on Lady Holy Church's formulations. The lowly plowman, in his first appearance, offers the well-meaning but confused folk of the field the directions that were given him by "Conscience and kynde wit" (B.V.539). They involve a long "signpost allegory"[6] of the moral law, leading to the "court" of Truth, surrounded by a "moot . . . of mercy," and supported by pillars of Penance, prayers, and alms-deeds. The "gateward" is Grace, with his man "amende-yow":

> "Biddeþ amende-yow meke hym til his maister ones
> To wayuen vp þe wiket þat þe womman shette
> Tho Adam and Eue eten apples vnrosted:
> *Per Euam cunctis clausa est et per Mariam virginem iterum patefacta est;*
> For he haþ þe keye and þe cliket þou3 þe kyng slepe.
> And if grace graunte þee to go in in þis wise
> Thow shalt see in þiselue truþe sitte in þyn herte
> In a cheyne of charite as þow a child were,
> To suffren hym and segge no3t ayein þi sires wille."
>
> (B.V.601–8)

Elizabeth Salter calls attention, quite rightly, to the abrupt shift of perspective in the last four lines. Though she gives the lines a mystical interpretation which seems to me mistaken, she does make the valuable observation that they clearly anticipate the *Vita de Dobet*: "As confirmation of what he is learning about divine love and truth, [Will] is allowed to witness the Crucifixion and the Harrowing of Hell; the gates are indeed opened to him, by grace, as he *sees* Truth bound by charity, Christ willingly sacrificed in love, so that he may gain entry to man's heart."[7] Here, as in the description of Truth as a

6. The phrase is John Lawlor's, in *Piers Plowman: An Essay in Criticism* (New York: Barnes and Noble, 1962), pp. 35, 56.
7. Elizabeth Zeeman (Salter), "Piers Plowman and the Pilgrimage to Truth," *Essays and Studies*, n.s., 11 (1958):1–16. The article appeared under

"kynde knowyng," the mystery of the Incarnation seems to be implied in some immediate way by our good works. We are now given a little more of the doctrinal basis of this implication with the mention of the sacrament of Penance and Grace. With the Incarnation and Redemption, Christ brought back to human nature the grace which transforms our natural good works into supernatural acts. Without this grace man's good works have only earthly meaning. With it they gain entry into heaven, for Grace "haþ þe keye and þe cliket." The channels of this grace to men are the sacraments, and by receiving them men participate in the Incarnation, which is thus an historical fact and a continuing presence in history. Because of the Incarnation and its consequent grace, truth has the double meaning we have seen in the speeches of Lady Holy Church and Piers.

The double aspect of truth, as the goal and the impetus toward the goal, lies behind other psychological descriptions in the poem which do not make use of the term itself. In Passus IX, the personification Wit gives a roundabout answer to the dreamer's question about where Do-well, Do-bet, and Do-best live:

> "Sire Dowel dwelleþ," quod Wit, "noȝt a day hennes
> In a Castel þat kynde made of foure kynnes þynges.
> Of erþe and Eyr it is maad, medled togideres,
> Wiþ wynd and wiþ water wittily enioyned.
> Kynde haþ closed þerInne, craftily wiþalle,
> A lemman þat he loueþ lik to hymselue.
> *Anima* she hatte; to hir haþ enuye
> A proud prikere of Fraunce, *Princeps huius mundi,*
> And wolde wynne hire awey wiþ wiles if he myȝte.
> Ac kynde knoweþ þis wel and kepeþ hire þe bettre,
> And haþ doon hire wiþ sire dowel, duc of þise Marches.
> . . . .
> Ac þe Constable of þe Castel þat kepeþ hem alle
> Is a wis knyȝt wiþalle, sire Inwit he hatte,
> And haþ fyue faire sones bi his firste wyue:

Professor Salter's former name. I am referring to a reprint in Edward Vasta, ed., *Middle English Survey* (Notre Dame, Ind.: University of Notre Dame Press, 1965), p. 206.

Sire Se-wel, and Sey-wel, and here-wel þe hende,
Sire werch-wel-wiþ-þyn-hand, a wiʒt man of strengþe,
And sire Godefray Go-wel, grete lordes alle.
Thise sixe ben set to saue þis lady *anima*
Til kynde come or sende and kepe hire hymselue."

(B.IX.1–11, 17–24)

I have omitted the definitions of Do-bet and Do-best, since my main interest at this point is in the Castle and in the Constable Inwit. The Castle is obviously man, and if there could be any doubt on that score we are told a little later that it is called *"caro"* which is "As muche to mene as man wiþ a Soule" (B.IX.50–51).

There has been some disagreement as to the identity of Inwit. Greta Hort and Randolph Quirk agree that it cannot mean "conscience." Quirk, in a survey of external philological evidence, found that this sense, despite its famous occurrence in the *Ayenbite of Inwyt*, was comparatively rare. Internal evidence is against it, too; as Quirk points out, the presence of a separate character named Conscience makes it an unlikely redundancy.[8] Miss Hort has postulated, instead, that Inwit is the scholastic *sensus communis* which integrates the data of the separate external senses to form a composite sense image.[9] This is suggested by Inwit's five sons who work under him to protect Lady Anima, although one of these, "sire Godefray Go-wel," is not really a sense. Quirk, on the other hand, suggests that "inwit is 'intellect,' the *agens* aspect of *intellectus* in Thomist terms, and since the intellect is concerned with the apprehension of truth, it is therefore con-

8. Randolph Quirk, "Langland's Use of Kind Wit and Inwit," *Journal of English and Germanic Philology* 52 (1953):187–88. Skeat glosses *inwit* as "conscience" (*Parallel Texts*, 2:139). Willi Erzgräber, in *William Langlands Piers Plowman: Eine Interpretation des C-Textes* (Heidelberg: Carl Winter, 1957), p. 118, agrees essentially with Skeat, though claiming we should take "conscience" in a broader sense which would include the general normative faculty of synderesis. Elizabeth Kirk, in *The Dream Thought of Piers Plowman* (New Haven: Yale University Press, 1972), p. 108, identifies Inwit as "conscience and consciousness."

9. Hort, pp. 96–97. The difficulty over "sire Godefray Go-wel" may be obviated by the suggestion of Joseph S. Wittig, in " 'Piers Plowman' B, Passus IX–XII: Elements in the Design of the Inward Journey," *Traditio* 28 (1972): 217, that "the five sons are not simply the five senses, but the sensual powers of man considered precisely as ordered to higher ends while justly supplying the needs of man." Wittig cites as a probable source of Langland's whole image of the Castle of Caro the *Liber de spiritu et anima*, in J.-P. Migne, *Patrologiae Cursus Completus . . . Series Latina* (Paris: 1844–65, hereafter *PL*), vol. 40, cols. 807–8.

cerned with the distinction between true and false, good and evil; hence its functions can come near to, and be confused with, those of conscience."[10]

Quirk's suggestion seems to be more plausible because of the external evidence he adduces and because of the precise role that Langland gives to Inwit. First of all, the sons of Inwit all have a positive moral value implied in their names: See-*well* and Say-*well* and so on. The *sensus communis* is nondeliberative and amoral. Furthermore, Inwit guards and serves Anima, and, according to the dominant scholastic epistemology, the *sensus communis* cannot have any direct relationship with Anima, the immaterial soul.[11] The transition from sensitive and particular knowledge to intellectual cognition is made by the "active intellect"—or "the *agens* aspect of *intellectus*"—which "illumines" the phantasm, abstracts from it the "intelligible species," and impresses this on the passive intellect.[12] The mediating role of Inwit conforms more readily with this account than with any account of the *sensus communi*s, whose operations Langland omits or silently assumes.[13]

When Saint Thomas described part of the function of the active intellect as an "illumination" of the phantasm, he was using a loaded word.[14] Previous Christian thinkers had used the word to denote a special act of God which completes man's cognition. In other words, they placed all or part of the operations of the active intellect directly into the hands of God. Saint Augustine stands at the head of this tradition of "divine illumination," though his discussion was not

10. Quirk, p. 187.

11. According to Saint Thomas and his followers, the rational and spiritual soul cannot be affected directly by a material thing or by the phantasm formed by the senses, including the *sensus communis*. Even the opponent of this doctrine, Duns Scotus, who argued that the rational soul could directly intuit sensible particulars, did not put the *sensus communis* in the intermediating position occupied by Sir Inwit. See Frederick Copleston, *A History of Philosophy*, 7 vols. (Westminster, Md.: Newman Press, 1957), 2:388–97, 487–99.

12. Ibid., pp. 389–90. I am following Copleston's account very closely.

13. Langland's whole allegory compares rather closely with that of "Sawles Warde," the twelfth-century prose work based on Hugh of St. Victor's *De Anima*. There "Wit" (who may also be called "Inwit," depending on the reading of a difficult line) is the "huse-lauerd" of the house of man, controlling his foolish wife "Wil", and having as his exterior servants the five senses. There could be no question here of making this character a personification of conscience or the *sensus communis*. For the text, see J. A. W. Bennett and G. V. Smithers, eds., *Early Middle English Verse and Prose* (Oxford: Oxford University Press, 1966), pp. 246–61, and cf. notes on pp. 418–19.

14. See *Summa Theologiae* 1.85.1, *ad* 4.

couched in Aristotelian terms, and he was not interested in constructing a systemic epistemology. We can only infer the rough outline of such a system from remarks directed toward other ends, usually apologetic or controversial. Thus, in rejecting Platonic and Pythagorean theories of reminiscence, he proposes instead that the intellect perceives necessary truths such as those of geometry "by a sort of incorporeal light of an unique kind; just as the carnal eye sees the things that surround it in this corporeal light, being made receptive and adapted to this light."[15] The source of this light is God, and the perception of necessary truths is used elsewhere as evidence of His existence: "For both the earth and light are visible; but the earth cannot be seen unless illumined by the light. So, too, those things taught in the sciences, which everyone knows and concedes to be perfectly true without a doubt, cannot be known, we must suppose, unless they are illumined by some sort of sun of their own."[16] And this sun is God.

Saint Augustine's reflections on the process of knowing led him to a formulation of man's mind as the image of God in the Trinity, and this idea exercised a profound influence on later thinkers. God's triune image could be seen in the memory, intellect, and will, or in the self-consciousness by which "we are, and we know that we are, and we love that being and knowledge."[17] This last suggests passages we have discussed in Langland in the way it makes knowledge imply love.

Saint Augustine's greatest follower in the development of the theory of divine illumination was Saint Bonaventure. For him the activities of abstraction or "judgment"[18] were a persuasive proof of God's existence, so that every act of knowledge was charged with

15. ". . . sed potius credendum est mentis intellectualis ita conditam esse naturam, ut rebus intelligibilibus naturali ordine, disponente Conditore, subjuncta sic ista videat in quadam luce sui generis incorporea, quemadmodum oculus carnis videt quae in hac corporea luce circumadjacent, cujus lucis capax eique congruens est creatus." *De Trinitate* 12.15.24, in *PL* 42:1011.

16. "Nam et terra visibilis, et lux: sed terra, nisi luce illustrata, videri non potest. Ergo et illa quae in disciplinis traduntur, quae quisquis intelligit, verissima esse nulla dubitatione concedit, credendum est ea non posse intelligi, nisi ab alio quasi suo sole illustrentur." *Soliloquia* 1.8.15, in *PL* 32:877.

17. ". . . imaginem Dei, hoc est summae illius Trinitatis, agnoscimus. . . . Nam et sumus, et nos esse novimus, et id esse ac nosse diligimus." *De civitate Dei* 11.26, in *PL* 41:339; cf. ibid. 11.28, in *PL* 41:342, and *De Trinitate* 9.12.18, in *PL* 42:972.

18. Etienne Gilson notes that Bonaventure "uses indifferently in the same sense the Aristotelian expression *abstrahere* and the Augustinian *judicare*," and that this complicates his notion of abstraction; see *The Philosophy of Saint Bonaventure* (New York: Sheed and Ward, 1938), p. 399.

supernatural significance. Epistemology almost implied mysticism. He makes an explicit and quite beautiful connection between divine illumination and the soul's image of the Trinity in a commentary on the design of the Tabernacle in Exod. 26:35: "As the *lampstand* there sheds its light, even so, the light of truth is ever glowing on the face of our mind; which is to say that the image of the most blessed Trinity ever brightly shines upon it."[19] God *is* His light, so His illumination of our minds shows in His reflected image.

Etienne Gilson, in his study of Bonaventure, describes the precise degree of divine participation involved in the illumination of the intellect: "The corporeal creature, as a mere vestige of God, requires His cooperation only as creator and conserver; the human soul, an express resemblance of God, assimilable to Him by a sort of supernaturalization which transfigures it, requires from God that which alone, by its divine quality, can make it acceptable to Him; but between these two is the human soul considered as an image which requires by reason of its status a divine co-operation more intimate than that of conservation, although less intimate than that of grace. Such precisely is the part played by divine illumination in relation to knowledge through the eternal principles. It does not simply sustain it as a cause, and it does not transfigure it from within as does a grace, but it moves it from within as a hidden object."[20] Thus divine illumination is a special act of God, though it is less than the act by which we are brought to mystical contemplation in this life or to the Beatific Vision in the next. Our intellect and its operations differ from the movement of the soul to God, but only as an image differs from a likeness.

Bonaventure's great contemporary Saint Thomas gave a different sense to "illumination." His Aristotelianism and his more consistent exposition of secondary causality involved, as Frederick Copleston says, "the rejection of the theory of divine illumination or rather the interpretation of divine illumination as equivalent to the natural light of the intellect with the ordinary and natural concurrence of God."[21] This was consistent with Thomas's formal distinction between philos-

---

19. *Journey of the Mind to God (Itinerarium mentis in Deum)* 3.1, in *The Works of Bonaventure*, trans. José de Vinck, 4 vols. (Paterson, N.J.: St. Anthony's Guild Press, 1960–), 1:28. Other passages dealing with divine illumination are *Journey of the Mind to God* 2.9 and *De scientia Christi* 4. ad 5, 6, in *Opera Omnia* (Quaracchi, 1891), 5:25.

20. Gilson, *The Philosophy of Saint Bonaventure*, p. 401.

21. Copleston, 2:426.

ophy and theology, a distinction which is foreign to the Augustinian approach, as was the related distinction between the natural and supernatural ends of man. It is true that for Thomas philosophy and the natural were insufficient in themselves and were completed by theology and the supernatural. But even to make them separately intelligible was a fundamental innovation.

We have suggested that Sir Inwit, in his separate but mediating relationship to Lady Anima, seems rather like the active intellect as described by Saint Thomas. But as we read further we find that this constable of the castle described by Wit is endowed with a dignity and authority which seems supernatural, a dignity which would be granted him by Augustine and Bonaventure:

> "Inwit and alle wittes enclosed ben þerInne
> For loue of þe lady *anima* þat lif is ynempned.
> Ouer al in mannes body heo walkeþ and wandreþ,
> Ac in þe herte is hir hoom and hir mooste reste.
> Ac Inwit is in þe heed and to þe herte he lokeþ,
> What *anima* is leef or looþ; he let hire at his wille,
> For after þe grace of god þe gretteste is Inwit."
>
> (B.IX.54–60)

The last line in particular seems quite close to Bonaventure's idea of God's relation to the intellect, "more intimate than that of conservation, although less intimate than that of grace." There is an interesting variation on this in the C-text, which puts more emphasis on the relationship of Inwit's counsel to the counsel of God:

> "By loue and leaute, ther-by lyueth *Anima*;
> And Lyf lyueth by Inwitt and lerynge of Kynde.
> Inwitt is in the hefd, as *Anima* in the herte,
> And muche wo worth hym that Inwitt mys-speyneth.
> For that is godes owen good, hus grace and hus tresoure,
> That meny lede leeseth thorw lykerouse drynke."
>
> (C.XI.171–76)

Here the usual relationship between B and C is reversed. Normally B makes the sweeping statements and takes the liberties that metaphor allows; then C makes the distinctions and qualifications that discursive statements of doctrine demand. But in this passage B is precise

and circumspect, placing Inwit "after þe grace of god," while C is
daring and says that Inwit *is* God's grace, pushing illumination in the
direction of deification.

Just preceding this passage in B there is an account of man's creation in God's image, a subject as closely relevant to the illumination of
the intellect for Langland as it is for the theologians of the Augustinian tradition. Wit has told the dreamer, in lines already quoted,
that the five sons of Inwit have been set to protect Anima "Tyl kynde
come or sende and kepe hire hymselve." The dreamer asks who Kind
is, and receives this answer:

> "Kynde," quod he, "is creatour of alle kynnes beestes,
> Fader and formour, þe first of alle þynges.
> And þat is þe grete god þat gynnyng hadde neuere,
> Lord of lif and of liȝt, of lisse and of peyne.
> Aungeles and alle þyng arn at his wille
> Ac man is hym moost lik of marc and of shape.
> For þoruȝ þe word þat he warp woxen forþ beestes,
> And al at his wil was wrouȝt wiþ a speche,
> *Dixit & facta sunt,*
> Saue man þat he made ymage to hymself,
> And Eue of his ryb bon wiþouten any mene.
> For he was synguler hymself and seide *faciamus*
> As who seiþ, 'moore moot herto þan my word oone;
> My myȝt moot helpe forþ wiþ my speche.'
> Right as a lord sholde make lettres; if hym lakked parchemyn,
> Thouȝ he wiste to write neuer so wel, and he hadde a penne,
> The lettre, for al þe lordshipe, I leue, were neuere ymaked.
> And so it semeþ by hym þere he seide in þe bible
> *Faciamus hominem ad imaginem nostram;*
> He moste werche wiþ his word and his wit shewe.
> And in þis manere was man maad þoruȝ myȝt of god almyȝty,
> Wiþ his word and werkmanshipe and wiþ lif to laste.
> And þus god gaf hym a goost of þe godhede of heuene
> And of his grete grace graunted hym blisse,
> Lif þat ay shal laste, and al his lynage after."[22]

(B.IX.26–49)

---

22. The text is corrupt in all MSS. Donaldson and Kane's text differs
notably from Skeat's (B.IX.26–47), and the reader may wish to compare the
two. The influence of Christian exemplarism, discussed here, is clear in both.

The last sixteen lines were omitted in the C-text, and the reader might feel inclined to thank Langland for this revision. The extended conceit is obscure, and seems internally inconsistent. The lines are worth our attention, though, because they attempt to appropriate a peculiar refinement in the doctrine of divine illumination.

Wit makes a distinction between the creation of man and that of other creatures. All others were made with a speech, *"Dixit & facta sunt,"* the speech being, of course, *"Fiat ———,"* which follows *"Dixit"* in the Vulgate Genesis. Man's creation was different because then God said *"faciamus."*[23] This different usage is somehow explained by the analogy of a lord trying to write without a parchment. Man, or something involved exclusively in man's creation, is to God as the paper is to that lord. He or it makes God's wit show, as a paper makes the lord's thought visible, as in an order or a plan. All this is somehow bound up with the idea that man was made in the image of God.

One tradition which may lurk in the obscurities of this passage is the Christian version of Platonic exemplarism. The tradition was popularized by Augustine, but many more proximate sources can be adduced. It takes as its point of departure *fiat, factum est,* and *fecit—* nearly the same words as those Langland plays on here—and finds in them three distinct phases in the process of Creation. Hugh of Saint Victor gives a good summary of the theory:

> Just as a man, when he has conceived something in his mind, draws an example of it externally, so that what was known only to him may be seen plainly by others, and afterwards, to make it still more evident, explains in words how the thing drawn as an example matches his idea of it; so, too, God, wishing to show his invisible Wisdom, drew its example in the mind of the rational creature [i.e., in the minds of angels], and next, by making the corporeal creature, showed the rational creature an

23. One popular explanation, as I note below, was that God used the plural to refer to His triune aspect. Skeat apparently follows the tradition, finding in the pen and parchment metaphors for the Son and Holy Ghost. This follows in part from his reading of lines 38–39: "Riȝte as a lorde sholde make lettres and hym lakked parchemyn,/Though he couth write neuere so wel ȝif he had no penne." An objection to the Trinity reference is that we cannot tell which of the two Persons is pen and which is parchment. There is no clear differentiation of function as there usually is in discussions of the Trinity. Instead the *common* function of pen and parchment, to make thought visible, is stressed here. See *Parallel Texts,* 2:140.

external example of what it itself contained within. Thus, the rational creature was made in first place and in likeness of the divine Idea, with nothing mediating between them. The corporeal creature, however, was made in the likeness of the divine Idea through the mediation of the rational creature.

For this reason, the book of Genesis, speaking of the angels under the appellation "light," says: "God said: Let there be light. And the light came to be." Concerning all the other works of God, however, it says: "God said: Let it be. And it was so"—and then it adds, "And God made it." For the angelic nature first existed in the divine Idea as a plan, and then afterwards it began to subsist in itself through creation. The other creatures, however, first existed in the Idea of God; next, they were made in the knowledge of the angels; and finally they began to subsist in themselves. When, therefore, Genesis says, "God said: Let it be," [*Dixit: fiat*] this refers to the divine Mind. And when it says, "And it was so," [*factum est*] this refers to the angelic intellect. And when it says, "And God made it," [*fecit*] it refers to the actuality of things.[24]

What subsists in the minds of the angels is the intelligible species or "kind" of each corporeal creature. Hence, the source of these intelligible species is the "Kind" par excellence. Langland's choice of this name for God in Wit's speech is perhaps one indication of his debt to exemplarism.

The place given by Hugh to angels in the original process of creation was assigned by others to man in the comprehension of creation. We can see here the same tendency of thought which pushed the active intellect in the direction of mystical contemplation. Saint Bonaventure tells us that "in the state of innocence, when the image had not yet been distorted," or—preserving the common distinction—

24. Hugh of Saint Victor, *The Didascalicon*, trans. Jerome Taylor (New York: Columbia University Press, 1961), p. 156. The Latin text is in *Hugonis de Sancto Victore Didascalicon De Studio Legendi: A Critical Text*, ed. Brother Charles Henry Buttimer, M.A. (Washington, D.C.: Catholic University Press, 1939), pp. 134–35. This passage appears as an introduction to the treatise in a number of MSS, but it is clear that this was not Hugh's placement. Where, or whether, he would have placed it in the *Didascalicon* is uncertain. See Buttimer, pp. xvi–xvii, and Taylor, p. 152. On the doctrine, cf. Augustine *De Genesi ad Litteram* 2.6–8, 4.29, 31, in *PL* 34:267–70, 315, 316; *De civitate Dei* 11.9, in *PL* 41:323–25.

when the *likeness* had not lost its pristine clarity, "but was conformed to God through grace, the book of creation sufficed to enable man to perceive the light of divine Wisdom. He was then so wise that, seeing all things in themselves [*fecit*], he also saw them in their proper genus [*factum est*] as well as in God's creating Art [*Dixit: fiat*]. For this accords with the triple manner in which creatures exist: in matter, that is, in their own nature; in the created intellect, and in the eternal Art."[25] Before original sin, then, man was not only an image and likeness of God; he was, in his act of knowledge, an imitation of the whole process of creation, played backwards, as it were. As he looked forward and outward on the corporeal world, his mind, illuminated by God, derived the proper genus of what he saw, just as the angels did, and then saw through the genus the Eternal Art which is identical with God Himself. Furthermore, the drama of creation is expressed with particular intensity in man because he is composed of its second and third terms, being both rational and corporeal. When sin darkens our likeness to God, we lose this ability to perceive the source of the world and of the operations by which we know it. But as we free ourselves from sin and grow in grace, the light from behind grows and transforms the seeing and doing that lie before us. Then, in the most profound sense, we see well, say well, hear well, work well with our hands, and go well.

This seems to be part of what lies behind Langland's conceit, but his use of *faciamus* indicates a variation. The lines tell us that when God said *faciamus* he was indicating that creating man called for some extraordinary effort. A simple word to the mediating angelic agent (*Dixit: fiat* ———) was enough for beasts, but man must be made "wiþouten any mene." *Faciamus*, the first person plural, occurs in the Vulgate only at the creation of man and may simply reproduce an inconsistency in the Hebrew where God is sometimes given a singular title, *Yahweh*, and sometimes the plural *Elohim*.[26] Latin com-

---

25. *The Breviloquium* 2.12.4, in *The Works of Bonaventure*, 2:105. The bracketed words represent what I hope is a pardonable subterfuge. In the sentence that follows this passage, Bonaventure orders the three verb forms this way: *fiat*, divine Idea or Eternal Art; *fecit*, rational creature; *factus est*, corporeal creature. This has the same significance as Hugh's formula, but it is in a different order. I felt my exposition was complicated enough without making this adjustment in the course of it. Langland follows Hugh's order.

26. See the note to Gen. 1:26 in The Jerusalem Bible (Garden City, N.Y.: Doubleday, 1966), where a consultation with angels or other heavenly powers is suggested as an alternative interpretation.

mentators misunderstood this and gave various explanations for the plural verb, among the most popular being that God referred to Himself in his triune aspect when engaged in the creation of the one earthly creature who would bear his triune image.[27] If Langland knew this explanation, he chose not to use it. The plural subject of *faciamus* for him is God's "myȝt" and "speche," and this odd reading seems to be his own.

This apparently original reading of the Latin illustrates a traditional doctrine also found in Dante's *Paradiso*, and we might approach Langland's exposition by way of Dante's. In Canto VII Beatrice explains why God became man to redeem fallen humanity. Her argument is based mainly on Saint Anselm's *Cur Deus Homo*, and in the course of it she explains that man, before original sin, was immortal, and that this immortality was the result of the manner of his creation.

> Ciò che da lei sanza mezzo distilla
>   non ha poi fine, perché non si move
>   la sua imprenta quand'ella sigilla.
> Ciò che da essa sanza mezzo piove
>   libero è tutto, perché non soggiace
>   alla virtute delle cose nove.
>
>   (VII.67–72)[28]

[Whatever distills from It (the Divine Goodness) without intermediary has no end afterward because Its imprint is not removed once it is stamped in. Whatever rains down from this without intermediary is wholly free, because it is not subject to the power of the new things (i.e., the stars).]

Dante finds this understandable as regards the soul, but what of the body? Is it not made of corporeal elements which common experience tells us must pass away? Beatrice concedes that these elements are corruptible because subject to the secondary causality of the stars, but goes on to suggest, rather elliptically, the reason why man, body and soul, is a special case:

27. Cf. Augustine *Confessions* 13.22, in *PL* 32:858–59; *De Genesi ad Litteram* 3.19.29, in *PL* 34:291–92.
28. *Paradiso*, a cura di Natalino Sapegno (Firenze: "La Nuova Italia" Editrice, 1957).

ma vostra vita sanza mezzo spira
    la somma beninanza, e la innamora
    di sé, sí che poi sempre la disira.
E quinci puoi argomentare ancora
    vostra resurrezion, se tu ripensi
    come l'umana carne fessi allora
che li primi parenti intrambo fensi.

(VII.142–48)

[But the Supreme Goodness breathes forth your life without
intermediary, and enamors it of Itself so that the soul desires It
forever after. And hence you can infer now your own
resurrection, if you consider how the human flesh was made
when the first parents were both formed.]

The mode of the fleshly creation of Adam and Eve is that recounted
in Genesis 2:7: "Then the Lord God formed man of dust from the
ground, and breathed into his nostrils the breath of life; and man became a living being." His word alone was not enough. He put His
hand to the task of shaping the dust. " 'My myȝt moot helpe forþ
wiþ my speche' . . . He moste werche wiþ his word and his wit
shewe." For Langland, as for Dante, the conjunction of God's "word"
with His "werkmanshipe" meant that man was endowed "wiþ lif to
laste." Both poets link man's immortality to his being "moost lik"
God "of marc and of shape," and to his being made "wiþouten any
mene."[29]

Let us return to that image of the pen and parchment. It seems
clearly related to Hugh of Saint Victor's description of mediate creation through the angels, which he compares to a man drawing out a
plan or blueprint of his conception, so as to render it visible to others.

---

29. Saint Thomas Aquinas makes substantially the same point in *Summa
Theologiae* 1.91.2, *respondeo*. He links this with the general resurrection of
the body in 1.91.2, *ad* 1. The doctrine is also found in Saint Ambrose *Hexae-
meron* 6.7. 40–43 (*PL* 14:272–74), where the creation of men without the
angels' help is connected with man's status as the image of God; and in
Augustine *De Genesi ad Litteram* 9.15.26 (*PL* 34:403–4), where emphasis is
placed on God's direct creation of Eve as well as Adam. Joseph Wittig points
out that the involvement of both God's "word" and "werkemanschip" in man's
creation suggests man's duty both to know and to love (and thus to practice)
God's law. He cites the parallel drawn in the anonymous treatise *De Spiritu et
Anima* (*PL* 40:805), between God's creative *sermo* and *opera* and the human
obligation to *intelligere* and *diligere* ("Inward Journey," p. 223).

God's urge to show what is in His mind is expressed more strikingly in Langland with the quick, deft sketch of a frustrated lord whose literacy, however advanced and hard won, is rendered useless by the want of a parchment. We seem to hear in Langland's tone the mixture of sympathy and satisfaction with which a commoner might view the noble's share in the common curse of absentmindedness: "The lettre, *for al þe lordshipe*, I leue, were neuere ymaked." When God creates man by means of His "word and werkmanshipe," one surprising re-sult is the resolution of this problem. In making man He makes "his wit shewe." The simile of the parchment which suggests God's rela-tionship to angels in Hugh of Saint Victor describes His relationship to men in Langland. Like Saint Bonaventure, Langland seems to put men in a position analogous to that of the angels, between material creation and the Creator, but he does so in a way peculiarly his own. In Bonaventure we see God's beneficent light flooding the grateful human mind after its arduous climb from the cognition of sensible particulars to their source in the divine Idea. In Langland, we see God Himself, at first frustrated, then rejoicing in a task of unaccustomed difficulty, gratefully giving eternal life to His finest work, the image of Himself in whom at last His wit is rendered visible.

As I noted before, Langland drops this passage in the C-text. What-ever his motives, he was consistent enough to drop another passage which seems to share the theme of God's delight in His last creation. Some fifty lines after the passage we have discussed, Wit condemns those who

> "spille speche þat spire is of grace
> And goddes gleman and a game of heuene.
> Wolde neuere þe feiþful fader his fiþele were vntempred
> Ne his gleman a gedelyng, a goere to tauernes."
>
> (B.IX.103–6)

The idea of speech as God's fiddle is quite close to the metaphor of the pen and parchment. In both cases the divine Idea is made public and sensible—God makes "his wit shewe"—and in both cases God can almost be said to be fulfilling himself in man. So it follows that speech is a "spyre of grace" just as Inwit is most precious "after the grace of god," and the misuse of either is something like a sacrilege. The term "spyre of grace" actually sounds like a description of a sacrament. There is, in addition to this suggestion of the sacramental, a pleasing sense of play in the description of speech as "goddes gleman and a game of heuene," as if God felt an exuberance in His creativity, and man's highest vocation was to be its joyous, singing expression. This imagery, the omission of which is a sad loss in the C-text, is closely related to the minstrel imagery which, as Donaldson has shown, Langland reduced in each revision lest he be misunderstood in a world where the more typical minstrel was "a gedelyng, a goere to tauernes."[30]

The sense of God's self-fulfillment in man, and the mixing of the sacramental and the intellectual in a common sense of play are basic and recurring elements in Langland. To a great extent they create that special tone of voice which sustains us through so much that is strange and bewildering in his poem and which invests its most visionary moments with such surprisingly antic humor. From this vantage point let us look backward and forward to just two of the passages that bring up these themes in somewhat similar tones. Lady Holy Church, in her instructions to Will, spoke of the delight of "Loue," or God the Son, in His newfound agility—"portatif and persaunt as þe point of a nedle"—after He had taken on man's flesh and blood. And shortly after Wit's speech Dame Study will lament the fallen state of minstrelsy (B.X.39ff.), which seems related to the fallen state of learning in some way so obvious to her that she need not explain it. Once again, Langland seems to have lost the connection in his own mind when he did the C revision, and so he drops most of this.

In one other change, though, the C-text gives a valuable reminder of how Wit's speech relates to what has gone before. Just after the passage in which Inwit is likened to the grace of God, in B Wit condemns those who misrule Inwit and so serve the devil, contrasting them with "alle þat lyuen good lif" and "are lik to god almyȝty" (B.IX.65). Langland's restatement of this in C is indirect and allusive: "Every man that hath Ynwitt and hus hele bothe, / Hath tresour ynow in treuthe to fynde with hym-selue" (C.XI.180–81). This return to the language in which Lady Holy Church extolled truth as the best treasure places Inwit very nicely in the context of the whole poem. It provides another instance of how God is both the goal and the impetus toward the goal. In its search for God the active intellect

30. *C-Text*, pp. 136–55; he cites the same passage on p. 148. On speech as a duty of man by which he communicates knowledge gained from God, see Thomas Aquinas *Summa Theologiae* 2–2.77, *ad* 1.

perceives His image in the very act of searching. Truth is at once transcendent and immanent, and man, in tracing its locus, becomes "a god by þe gospel, a grounde and o lofte." Of course, this account is partial, coming as it does from Wit, who is the intelligence considered as a whole. The only misruling of Inwit he can conceive is a derangement through too much food or drink. It remains for Study, his domineering wife, to show how the intellect can be abused through its choice of objects and motives even when it is working with full clarity and strength. Inwit is not "tresour *ynow* in treuthe," but it is a necessary, divinely endowed component in the image and likeness of God.

One more psychological passage which exploits the double aspect of truth has been treated extensively and well by Greta Hort and Professor Donaldson, and my own remarks on it derive much from theirs.[31] This is the passage in Passus XVI which involves the Tree of Charity and the personification *Liberum-Arbitrium*. In B this is a dream within a dream, which interrupts the speech of Anima and has Piers Plowman for its central expositor. In the C-text (beginning at C.XVII.158) the passage is a continuation of the Haukyn episode and has for its central expositor *Liberum-Arbitrium*, who replaces both Anima and Piers. The scene is extremely complex, and it could be argued that it is not under the complete control of its author. I do not intend to treat it exhaustively here; one particularly important element, the role of Piers in the B-text, I will reserve for later discussion. A point which is relevant to the previous discussions of truth, and Inwit, though, is the intersection of the divine and human spheres of operation in the faculty of free will, an intersection for which Donaldson suggested a precedent in Bernard of Clairvaux and his followers.

In the B-text, the dreamer asks "what charite is to mene" (B.XVI. 3). Anima explains that it is the fruit of a tree called Patience which grows "Amyddes mannes body" (B.XVI.14) where it is kept by *Liberum-Arbitrium*, a tenant under Piers the Plowman. When the dreamer hears that name he swoons into a deeper dream where he stands before the Tree of Charity and has for his instructor Piers himself. The tree is supported by three props taken from another tree called Trinity, lest the Tree of Charity be blown by the three winds of

31. Hort, pp. 113–15; Donaldson, *C-Text*, pp. 180–96.

the world, the flesh, and the devil. As Piers explains, when the wind of the world threatens the tree, "Thanne with þe firste pil I palle hym doun, *potencia dei patris.*" When the wind of the flesh comes, "Thanne sette I to þe secounde pil, *sapiencia dei patris,* / That is þe passion and þe power of oure prince Iesu" (B.XVI.30, 36–37). But when the devil comes, the expected recourse to the Holy Ghost is delayed and stated in the most roundabout way:

> "Ac *liberum arbitrium* letteþ hym som tyme,
> That is lieutenaunt to loken it wel bi leue of myselue:
> *Videatis qui peccat in spiritum sanctum, numquam remittetur*
>   & c; *Hoc est idem qui peccat per liberum arbitrium non*
>   *repugnat.*
> Ac whan þe fend and þe flessh forþ wiþ þe world
> Manacen bihynde me, my fruyt for to fecche,
> Thanne *liberum arbitrium* laccheþ þe þridde planke,
> And palleþ adoun þe pouke pureliche þoru3 grace
> And help of þe holy goost, and þus haue I þe maistrie."
>   (B.XVI.46–52)

There are several variations from the norm here. First, Piers, who is about to assume the role of Christ's human nature, does not wield the stick himself as he had done in the first two cases, but delegates the job to his tenant, a faculty of human nature, *Liberum-Arbitrium.* Second, as already noted, the mention of the Person of the Trinity is delayed, and so the human collaboration is emphasized. Third, the Holy Ghost does not have a Latin title as the Father and the Son do; instead, the Latin name of the human faculty is placed in a position exactly parallel to "*potencia dei patris*" and "*sapiencia dei patris.*" Finally, there is a Latin interpolation which sets up an odd equation between the sin against the Holy Ghost and a sin through free will. The effect of all this is to make *Liberum-Arbitrium* and the Holy Ghost work in a unison which makes them almost indistinguishable.

Miss Hort calls our attention to some lines near the end of Passus XVI, where Abraham, in the role of Faith, describes the Trinity:

> "So is þe fader forþ with þe sone and fre wille of boþe,
> *Spiritus procedens a patre & filio & c,*
> Which is þe holy goost of alle, and alle is but o god."
>   (B.XVI.223–24)

Here the Holy Ghost is the free will of God, and so the relationship of God and man is once again that of exemplar and image. As Miss Hort says, "The difficulty of reconciling the two conceptions is much the same difficulty as we met at the very beginning, where Truth was used to signify two different aspects of the same thing." Free will is raised to the highest importance among man's rational faculties, so that it is virtually "the Holy Ghost in man, helped by the Holy Ghost outside man, which finally leads man to salvation."[32]

In the C-text the importance of *Liberum-Arbitrium* is further emphasized by having him replace Piers entirely. The second tree called Trinity is eliminated, and the Tree of Charity is renamed *Ymago Dei*.[33] The awkward inconsistency in the defense against the third of the "wicked winds" is removed:

> Thenne fondeth the Feende my frut to destruye,
>
> .   .   .   .
>
> Thenne palle ich a-downe the pouke with the thridde shoryere,
> The whiche is *Spiritus-sanctus* and soth-fast byleyue,
> And that is grace of the Holy Gost; and thus gat ich the mastrye.
>
> (C.XIX,43, 50–52)

Since Piers is no longer present to delegate part of his authority to his tenant and keep part himself, *Liberum-Arbitrium* has a remarkable extension of power. This faculty now commands the aid of all three Persons of the Trinity, and he undergoes the translation that B reserved for Piers as the entire human nature of Christ. This occurs in B when the devil carries off the patriarchs and prophets who fall from the tree:

> And Piers for pure tene þat a pil he lauȝte;
> He hitte after hym, happe how it myȝte,
> *Filius* by þe fader wille and frenesse of *spiritus sancti,*
> To go robbe þat Rageman and reue the fruyt fro hym.
>
> (B.XVI.86–89)

32. *Religious Thought*, p. 115.
33. Smith, in *Traditional Imagery*, p. 60, suggests that *Ymago Dei*, called an *ympe* (C.XIX.6), is not synonymous with the "tre . . . Trewe loue" (C. XIX.9) as Skeat suggests (*Parallel Texts*, 2:235), but is a divine shoot grafted onto the tree of man. This is difficult syntactically, but the idea of grafting as a symbol for the intersection of the divine and the human has traditional sup-

The narrative then shifts suddenly to an account of the Annunciation, the Incarnation, and the rest of the life of Christ. In C the idea of the Holy Ghost as the free will of God is taken from its place near the end of the Passus and brought forward to accomplish the literal deification of *Liberum-Arbitrium*:

> Thenne meuede hym mod *in maiestate dei,*
> That *Libera-Uoluntas-Dei* lauhte the myddel shoriere,
> And hitte after the fende, happe hou hit myghte.
> *Filius,* by the faders wil, flegh with *Spiritus Sanctus,*
> To ransake that rageman and reue hym hus apples,
> That fyrst man deceyuede thorgh frut and false by-heste.
>
> (C.XIX.118–23)

In this emphasis upon will Langland is invoking a tradition different from the cognitive one of "divine illumination," though it is related. Donaldson, in discussing the relations of B and C in this episode, suggests that Saint Bernard or one of his followers may be the doctrinal source. For Bernard the free will is the seat of God's image; it is also the loving faculty, the seat of charity, which, as Anima told Will in the B-text, is "a childissh þyng . . . Wiþouten fauntelte or folie a fre liberal wille" (B.XV.149–50).[34] Donaldson remarks that the last phrase is "almost . . . a punning translation of *liberum arbitrium,*"[35] and the lines were eliminated when C reassigned Anima's speech to *Liberum-Arbitrium*. This change from the cognitive emphasis of Lady Holy Church and Wit has as a corollary an explicit emphasis upon grace in this intersection of the divine and human spheres of operation.

In shifting from the cognitive to the affective in locating the image of God, the passage retains some vital links with the earlier passages, particularly in the curious transformations of the Tree of Charity itself, which lead up to the transformation of Piers in B and *Liberum-Arbitrium* in C. The tree grows "Amyddes mannes body" in a garden made by God (or, as C.XIX.4 has it, in "a contree, *Cor-hominis* hit

---

port. Perhaps an "engrafted tree," like the "ympe-tree" of *Sir Orfeo,* line 70 (ed. A. J. Bliss [Oxford: Oxford University Press, 1954]), is what Langland had in mind.

34. See Saint Bernard *De gratia et libero arbitrio 9* (*PL* 182:1016), a passage cited by Donaldson, *C-Text,* p. 189. See, also, Gilson, *The Mystical Theology of Saint Bernard* (New York: Sheed and Ward, 1940), pp. 45ff.

35. *C-Text,* p. 193.

hyhte"). Its root is mercy; its trunk is pity; its leaves are loyal words, the laws of Holy Church; and its blossoms are obedient speech. Its name is Patience and its fruit is Charity (B.XVI.4–8), a fulfillment of the identification of patient poverty and charity which the preceding Passūs have developed.[36] All this is quite intelligible, if a bit ungainly. The tree is the internal source of virtue in the individual man, and all the virtues are simply different kinds of charity. But a little later, when the dreamer asks Piers to describe the fruit of the tree, we are told that it grows in three kinds, each sweeter than the last: matrimony, widowhood, and virginity (B.XVI.67–72).[37] There is thus a shift from the individual to the social economy of charity, but both have the same central symbol, the tree that grows "Amyddes mannes body." When the dreamer asks to taste an apple from the tree a further complication is presented to us. For as Piers shakes the tree, the devil enters and bears off the fallen apples; and among them are "Adam and Abraham and Ysaye þe prophete, / Sampson and Samuel and Seint Iohan þe Baptist" (B.XVI.81–82). There is now a shift from the social to the historical economy of charity as Will and Piers collaborate in reenacting Adam's sin, "knocking down an apple in response to human curiosity and thus bringing death and the devil into the world."[38] The whole sweep of Old Testament history is compressed to an instant, to the shaking of a tree that grows "Amyddes mannes body" and is seen in a dream within a dream.[39] Once this widest possible perspective is attained we are ready for the abrupt bursting forth into the story of the Incarnation and Redemption, which transforms the individual man, society, and all of history in a single visitation of grace.

Let us return, briefly, to the speech of Lady Holy Church. There we saw how our "kynde knowyng" of the moral law implied in some immediate, alogical way the whole history of the Redemption. Truth teaches us that love is heaven's remedy, and that heaven was so heavy

36. In C.XIX.9 the tree's name is changed to "Trewe-loue."

37. C.XIX.58–104 expands this.

38. Kirk, p. 169. Professor Kirk does not speak of a collaboration of Will and Piers in reenacting Adam's sin, but this does follow from the fact that the "human curiosity" in question is Will's and from her own interesting suggestion that Will and Piers are related somewhat in the manner of the Yeatsian self and anti-self (p. 76).

39. M. W. Bloomfield, in "Piers Plowman and the Three Grades of Chastity" (*Anglia* 76 [1958]:245–53), discusses Langland's use of the tree as both "a schematic and a chronological symbol," and suggests a mixture here of Joachite historical thought with traditional teachings on chastity, both of which were embodied in symbolic trees.

with it that it fell to earth and took earth to itself in the Incarnation. Here the equivocation between truth and Truth, love and Love is deliberate. When Truth "comseþ by myght" in man's heart to become manifest in good deeds, its movement is one with that by which the Word was made flesh. This is true because of the presence of grace, of which Lady Holy Church is custodian. When Piers gives his exposition of the way to Truth through the Ten Commandments, he is bringing this movement to its conclusion. It ends where it began, in man's heart where Truth is found "In a cheyne of charite." The Incarnation happens again, or it *still* happens in some way that transcends the very history it informs and makes "again" meaningless. And its setting is at once history and a garden "Amyddes mannes body" in a country called "*Cor-hominis.*"

In Wit's speech on the Castle of Caro and Sir Inwit, we have seen how the first events of sacred history, particularly the creation, were directly related to the divine illumination of the intellect and the image of God in man's cognition. Langland appropriated some version of the exemplarist account of creation whereby the rational intellect of man comprehended and showed forth the divine Idea behind corporeal creation. The cognitive operations of man implied the events of sacred history up to but not including the Incarnation, because that event was a visitation of grace, whereas the divine endowment of the intellect is only greatest "after the grace of god." Thus it is that Wit's narrative passages all come from the Old Testament. Wit is witty enough to see beyond himself, though, as his closing definition of "Dobest" shows us:

> "And so comeþ dobest aboute and bryngeþ adoun mody,
> And þat is wikked wille þat many werk shendeþ,
> And dryueþ awey dowel þoruȝ dedliche synnes."
>
> (B.IX.208–10)

Wit knows that the ultimate struggle for man's soul is carried out in the will. When man is saved it will be because of the transformation of his free will—*liberum-arbitrium*—by the grace of the Incarnation. The movement from intellect to will parallels Lady Holy Church's extension of "kynde knowyng" into loving, and progression of the Old Testament into the New in Passus XVI.[40]

40. Smith notes that the tree of Jesse was commonly used in manuscript illuminations "to join matter traditionally connected with the old dispensation to matter traditionally connected with the new" (*Traditional Imagery*, p. 62).

The episode of the Tree of Charity and *Liberum-Arbitrium* has thus been well prepared for. It in turn prepares us for the climax of the poem, Passus XVIII (C. XXI), in which the central event of sacred history, the Redemption, is narrated with such easy brilliance and clarity that we share the poet's confidence that here at last he has resolved every issue, internal, external, social, and historical, that he has raised in the poem. What we see fully and explicitly in Passūs XVI–XVIII we have glimpsed fitfully in the earlier psychological passages where the Incarnation was seen as the ultimate ground and reward of the good life. Now, at the poem's climax, the narrative itself is an adequate symbol of the dreamer's inner peace.

3. The Social Dimension

In HIS STUDY of the A-text, T. P. Dunning suggests, rather tentatively, that the king who appears in Passūs III and IV "must be taken to signify not only Kingship in general and the King of England in particular, but also the individual man, or, more abstractly—and better, I think—the human will in general."[1] Nevill Coghill, in a discussion dealing mainly with the B-text, suggests that the king who is prophesied in some rather obscure eschatological passages later in the poem "is Christ at His Second Coming."[2] Both of these interpretations seem to me to be mistaken, but both are based on a sound perception of the strange nature of Langland's king. This problem involves us immediately in Langland's view of society, the field of folk between heaven and hell which, Langland hoped, could embody, in a corporate way and in time, that image of God which was the fruit of the Incarnation in the individual soul. Such an ambition, though Christian in origin, could come in conflict with the Christian vision of the City of God which perfects the Earthly City only by supplanting it and by ending time.

The circumstances of the trial of Meed in Passūs III and IV seem at first to demand the sort of internalizing reading that Father Dun-

---

1. *A-Text*, p. 101.
2. "The Pardon of Piers Plowman," *Proceedings of the British Academy* 30 (1944):244. The passages he discusses are B.VIII.100–110 (A.IX.90–100), and B.X.322–35.

ning gives them. Here, after all, we have a king, a fully human being,
sharing the stage equally with several personified internal faculties:

> The kyng callede Conscience and afterward Reson
> And recordede þat Reson hadde riȝtfully schewed,
>
> . . . .
>
> "I am redy," quod Reson, "to reste wiþ yow euere;
> So Conscience be of youre counseil kepe I no bettre."
> "I graunte gladly," quod þe kyng, "goddes forbode he faile!
> Als longe as I lyue lyue we togideres."
>
> (B.IV.171–72,192–95)

There is a problem of perspective here which does not arise in situations where the dreamer speaks with Conscience or Wit or any other
of the personified faculties. There his interlocutor is readily intelligible as a projection of himself, and the dialogue is actually a self-
examination. Even in the more complex situations where Conscience
addresses a third party while the dreamer looks on, the faculty can
be understood as an individual projection. Thus Conscience puts questions to the corpulent Master and to Hawkin which are implicitly the
dreamer's own. But in Passūs III and IV the situation is different.
Here the dreamer is not the emanating center of the action as he is
on his later search for Do-well. He is instead an onlooker; if he is on
the stage at all it is as one of the faceless crowd of commoners. Conscience, Reason, and the King are equidistant from him; and their
forms are present to the dreamer in the same way, with no distinction
made between person and personification. If the reader wants to make
sense of the scene, he is almost forced to internalize the king (as
Father Dunning does) or to externalize the faculties.

Several passages added to A in B give the king an eschatological
significance, and so lend plausibility to Coghill's reading. Conscience,
in refuting Meed, looks forward to a time when Reason will govern
the realms, and when "oon cristene kyng," whose advent will be
heralded by celestial signs, will "kepen vs echone" (B.III.289). When
the king takes Reason and Conscience into the court as counselors, it
seems as if he is about to become that "oon cristene kyng." Much
later in the poem, Clergy develops his dour definition of Do-best ("to
be boold to blame þe gilty, / Syþenes þow seest þiself as in soule
clene" [B.X.264–65]) into another prophecy of this super-king:

"Ac þer shal come a kyng and confesse yow Religiouses,
And bete yow, as þe bible telleþ, for brekynge of youre rule,
And amende Monyals, Monkes and Chanons,
And puten hem to hir penaunce, *Ad pristinum statum ire*;

. . . .

Ac er þat kyng come Caym shal awake,
Ac dowel shal dyngen hym adoun and destruye his myȝte."

(B.X.322–25, 334–35)

It is noteworthy that in C these lines are moved forward in the poem
and made a part of Reason's speech to the kingdom after he has been
made a counselor to the king.[3] This reinforces the potential identity
of the king of Passūs III and IV with the "oon cristene kyng." The
passage is also an example of what Morton Bloomfield calls "the
apocalyptic vision in all its glory."[4] Although Bloomfield's characterization of *Piers Plowman* as a "fourteenth-century apocalypse" is
somewhat too restrictive, he is quite correct in pointing out the close
connection between the social and the apocalyptic in Langland's
thought.

We might recall here the apparent inconsistencies which we discov-
ered in some of the psychological passages dealt with in chapter 2,
for they present problems which are complementary to the present
ones. In Lady Holy Church's speech and in Piers's directions for
finding Truth, our moral perception and good deeds found their prototype in the Incarnation; in a sense they *were* the Incarnation happen-
ing again. Wit's description of the Castle of *Caro* involved an idiosyncratic version of Christian exemplarism in which our cognition
found its prototype in the Creation, showing as in a mirror the "wit"
of the Creator. In the episode of the Tree of Charity and *Liberum-
Arbitrium*, the movement of our free will, aided by grace, against the
temptations of the world, the flesh, and the devil imitated the whole
sweep of sacred history from the Fall through the Incarnation, and
also contained within itself the image of the whole Christian society
in its three grades of perfection: marriage, widowhood, and virginity.

3. C.VI.169–80. Some of the apocalyptic elements are softened. Instead of
Cain's arising and fighting with Do-well, "Clerkus and holychurche shal be
clothed newe" (180).
4. *Apocalypse*, p. 121. On the political implications of medieval millenarianism, see Norman Cohn, *The Pursuit of the Millennium*, rev. ed. (New York:
Oxford University Press, 1970), esp. pp. 198–280.

In all these passages, events and figures that logically belong outside man are somehow incorporated within him. History and society find their proper life and home in a country called *Cor-hominis*.

Suppose now we reverse the process and let the movements of society and history imitate the movements of man's mind. Let the faculties and disciplines and forces which logically belong inside man be projected outside him. Conscience and Kind Wit and Reason now walk abroad among men, plead before the king, and win places at his side as counselors. The king, thus surrounded, does indeed begin to look like the human will, but not by a metaphor of Langland's. Instead, the metaphor is in the society that Langland posits. The king is the will of the commonwealth which ideally is formed to the image and likeness of man.

Let us take a further step in this reversal. The reduction of history to its image in man involves an abrogation of time. All of sacred history from the Fall to the Incarnation is compressed to the instant when Piers or *Liberum-Arbitrium* shakes the tree "Amyddes mannes body." The projection of man's image onto history at large, with its evolution of a human society, involves a complementary abrogation of time. When Reason and Conscience are fully projected into the exterior world of society, when they take their seats as counselors to the king, then time is no more; signs appear in the heavens:

"And er þis fortune falle fynde men shul þe worste
By sixe sonnes and a ship and half a shef of Arwes;
And þe myddel of a Moone shal make þe Iewes torne,
And Sarȝynes for þat siȝte shul synge *Gloria in excelsis &c,*
For Makometh and Mede myshappe shul þat tyme;
For *Melius est bonum nomen quam diuicie multe.*"[5]

(B.III.325–30)

Langland's kingdom, set up and tumbled down at different points in the poem, has the natural atemporality of an hypothesis. Like, say, the ideal state of Plato, it does not inhabit historical time. But there is another way in which it transcends history and time. Considered as an instance of the workings of grace, as a consequence of the historical moment of Incarnation and Redemption, Langland's kingdom is

5. The Latin text is Prov. 22:1.

an eschatological reality. Its advent marks the end of time and history. As we have seen, both the act of knowledge and the act of moral choice in man had crucial events associated with them, namely, the Creation and the Incarnation. Both associations followed, in different ways, from the fact that man was created in the image and likeness of God. The reformation of society in man's image is thus, by extension, its reformation in God's image. It has its own special moment in sacred history as well, the Second Coming, the last great visitation of grace to man, foreshadowed by the Incarnation and by the movements of the redeemed human will to God. Willy-nilly, it seems, the ideal king's separate identity is lost in the Person of the returning Christ. And yet Langland seems to have tried to keep them apart, drawing upon tendencies of thought in his time which sought to sanctify the kingdom of man without losing its secular character.

Langland's tableau of the ideal king surrounded by personified faculties and virtues has many precedents in medieval political thought which have been investigated recently by Ernst Kantorowicz. Medieval legalists commonly made a distinction between the king as public official and as private man, and they expressed this by the fiction of "the King's Two Bodies." In his "Body Natural," the king was a human being, subject to mortality and the infirmities of childhood, old age, disease, and sin. In his "Body Politic," he was immortal, exempt from human infirmities, and invisible and immaterial except as incarnated by the "Body Natural."[6] The doctrine solved some real problems in the definition of the king's authority, rendering it at once stable and distinct from any merely personal grandeur.[7]

As the incarnation of the Body Politic, the individual king was joined simultaneously and through space with his kingdom as head of the *corpus mysticum* of the commonwealth. It is thus that we first meet the king in *Piers Plowman*, with the constituents of his power clearly outside his person:

6. See Ernst Kantorowicz, *The King's Two Bodies: A Study in Mediaeval Political Theology* (Princeton: Princeton University Press, 1957), p. 7, for a succinct statement of the doctrine by the Elizabethan jurist Edmund Plowden.

7. On the last point, Kantorowicz points out how Parliament, in challenging Charles I in 1642, did not alter the terms of his reign or of their subjection, did not, in other words, have direct recourse to the modern doctrine that the governor receives his authority from the consent of the governed. Instead, they proceeded against the king in his "Body Natural" on behalf of the king in his "Body Politic." See pp. 20–23.

Thanne kam þer a kyng; knyȝthod hym ladde;
Might of þe communes made hym to regne.
And þanne cam kynde wit and clerkes he made
For to counseillen þe kyng and þe commune saue.

(B.Prol.112–15)[8]

The king was also joined continuously and through time with every
other king before and after him in his Body Politic, which was in-
stantly reincarnated in his successor upon his death.[9] Thus was established a kind of profane eternal principle modeled upon—and in some
way competing with—the sacred eternal principle of the Church.

This grandiose fiction had several curious ramifications. Since the
king in his Body Politic was a species, not a mere individual, he was
like an angel, since, according to some theologians, each angel, as
pure form unmixed with matter, was a species to himself.[10] Or he was
given the status, hardly less dignified, of a universal idea in the mind
of God, like "Justice" or "Truth" or "Reason." Legalists were fond
of decorating their technical treatises with dream visions of Reason,
Justice, Equity, and the like, enshrined in temples, endowed with
halos, and, sometimes, with the king in their midst as an equal, more
or less as Langland sees him at the end of Passus IV.[11] These exalted
beings were supratemporal and yet not eternal. A new category was
needed: they were "eviternal."[12] And they inhabited a theoretical
earthly paradise like that of Dante's *De Monarchia*, where this quasi-
theology of the Earthly City is drawn to its logical conclusion: "There
are two ends, therefore, which unerring Providence has proposed to
men: the beatitude of this life, which consists in the exercise of man's
own powers, and which is figured forth in the earthly Paradise; and
the beatitude of eternal life, which consists in the enjoyment of the
divine vision to which man's own powers cannot ascend unless helped
by divine light, and which is made intelligible by the heavenly Paradise. . . . On account of this, man has needed a twofold direction: to
wit, the supreme Pontiff who guides the human race to eternal life by

8. On this passage, see Donaldson, *C-Text*, pp. 88–111. For another statement of the king's status as head of the body of the commonwealth see B.
XIX.466–76.
9. See Kantorowicz, pp. 268–450, esp. 268–72.
10. See Saint Thomas Aquinas *Summa Theologiae* 1.50.4.
11. See Kantorowicz, pp. 107–12, 282, and (following p. 512) figs. 16b,
18a, 18b, 19, and 20.
12. Ibid., pp. 164, 171–72, 270–84.

revelation; and the Emperor who directs the human race to temporal happiness by the lessons of philosophy."[13] Though Dante retreats from this confident dualism in the *Commedia*, his strong sense of the prerogatives of secular rule still underlies his rage against Boniface VIII and those famous, mysterious prophecies of a king who will come and set all to rights.[14]

Dante's hoped-for king has some clear affinities with Langland's, but Langland did not go as far as Dante in the separation of Church and state. His theoretical statements are generally conservative. For him the *corpus mysticum* par excellence is the Church, and kingly authority is subordinate. We can gather this from Thought's explanation of the three "Do's" to the Dreamer. Do-well, he says, is the laity, and Do-bet the Clergy:

> Dobest is aboue boþe and bereþ a bisshopes crosse;
> Is hoked at þat oon ende to holde men in good lif.
> A pik is in þat potente to punge adown þe wikked
> That waiten any wikkednesse dowel to tene.
> And as dowel and dobet dide hem to vnderstonde,
> Thei han crowned a kyng to kepen hem alle,
> That if dowel and dobet dide ayein dobest
> And were vnbuxum at his biddyng, and bold to don ille,
> Thanne sholde þe kyng come and casten hem in prison,
> And putten hem þer in penaunce wiþoute pite or grace,
> But dobest bede for hem abide þer for euere.
>
> (B.VIII.96–106)[15]

13. "Duos igitur fines Providentia illa inenarrabilis homini proposuit intendendos; beatitudinem scilicet huius vitae, quae in operatione propriae virtutis consistit, et per terrestrem Paradisum figuratur; et beatitudinem vitae aeternae, quae consistit in fruitione divini aspectus ad quam propria virtus ascendere non potest, nisi lumine divino adiuta, quae per Paradisum coelestem intelligi datur. . . . Propter quod opus fuit homini duplici directivo, secundum duplicem finem: scilicet summo Pontifice, qui secundum revelata humanum genus perduceret ad vitam aeternam; et Imperatore, qui secundum philosophica documenta genus humanum ad temporalem felicitatem dirigeret." *De monarchia* 3.16, ed. E. Moore, with introduction by W. H. V. Reade (Oxford: Oxford University Press, 1916), pp. 375, 376.

14. Cf. *Inferno* 1.94ff.; *Purgatorio* 33.37ff. The suggestion that these prophecies refer to the Second Coming was made by R. E. Kaske, "Dante's 'DXV' and 'Veltro,'" *Traditio* 17 (1961):185–256. His arguments are supported by great learning, but they are not, I think, finally persuasive. See Robert Hollander's comments in *Allegory in Dante's Commedia* (Princeton: Princeton University Press, 1969), pp. 182–88, including notes.

15. The text is corrupt, and Donaldson and Kane's reading differs notably from Skeat's (B.VIII.94–102), following the A-Text (IX.86–96) more closely.

This sets up a rather complicated relationship between Church and state. The religious and laity choose a king—much as "Might of þe communes made hym to regne"—in order to keep *them* from doing harm to the official hierarchical Church. The king can punish them for doing "ayein dobest," but there is no legitimate way he can do "ayein dobest" himself. He is endowed with absolute power "holy kirke and clergie fro cursed men to defende" (B.XIX.467) and by that very endowment is rendered subject to the Church. Nevertheless, if Langland did not follow the ideal of kingship to Dante's conclusions, he seems to have been drawn emotionally in that direction. His constant and specific concern with social ills and their remedies seems almost to imply the possibility of an earthly paradise regained, if not by "man's own powers," by that mysterious enlargement of man's powers by which he becomes "a god by þe gospel, a grounde and o lofte." It is certainly true that he gives the vessel of this hope, the "oon cristene kyng," a visionary grandeur he never grants to pope or bishop.

Logically, though, the Earthly City must yield to the City of God, for him as for Saint Augustine. The sinful world is not to be redeemed, but supplanted. But the logic of Langland's vision is not always consistent with its emotional content. There is a specific density to his concern for the world which seems to make it a fit subject of redemption in his eyes. We are doing ill, he says, and we *could* be doing well. We abuse our individual consciences, reasons, kind wits, and thus block their emergence as corporate entities, as expressions of our wills united in the search for Truth. But our very possession of these faculties and our awareness of how their operations are transformed by the graces of the Incarnation argue the possibility of their emergence as counselors to the one Christian king, a king who rules not in heaven but on earth. There remains, however, the contradiction inherent in Langland's social thought. Every attempt to realize his vision of society's final redemption must turn into a vision of its end in apocalypse. For the orthodox Christian there is no other way. The fullness of time is the end of time. Signs appear in the heavens, and time redeemed is time no more.

This central irony of the poem's outlook blocks any attempt to read it as a subjective, mystical journey to contemplation. There is no mystical purgation of the senses in the poem and no *contemptus mundi*. The dreamer moves among internal faculties in the *Vita de Dowel*, but each of them trains his gaze steadily on the world outside.

Like Langland, they care intensely about that world and about its
institutions. From vantages further and further inside the dreamer,
Thought, Wit, Study, and Anima all look out and give detailed criticisms of a world which refuses to resolve itself into their corporate
image and the image of that Truth which is their exemplar.

Lady Holy Church said that "in þe herte . . . is þe heed and þe
heiȝe welle" of Truth. Piers the Plowman gave his laborious directions—through the Ten Commandments, past Grace the gate-ward,
and into the court of Truth—and the journey was found to end where
it began, in the heart of man. There Truth was found in a chain of
charity, Christ incarnate submitting to the bondage of His love for
man. The C-text reproduces this passage with a significant alteration:

> "And yf Grace graunte the to go yn in thys wise,
> Thow shalt se Treuthe sytte in thy selue herte,
> And solace thy soule and saue the fro pyne.
> Al-so charge Charyte a churche to make
> In thyn hole herte to herberghwen alle treuthe,
> And fynde alle manere folke fode to hure saules,
> Yf loue and leaute and owre lawe be trewe."

(C.VIII.254–60)

If the passage in B points to the Incarnation, this one looks beyond
that central event to its ultimate consequence, the sacred *corpus
mysticum*, the Heavenly City which is the remote aspiration of Piers's
barn of Unity. This is the Kingdom of Heaven that is within us, of
which every earthly kingdom is but a shadow or figure. But the presence of such a clear exemplar of social perfection within our hearts
during our lifetime begets inevitably a desire to give substance to the
shadow, to found a human society that embodies that social perfection here on earth. For Langland such a desire can be neither satisfied nor stilled. Not for him the equanimity of Socrates, who, when
faced with the objection that his ideal Republic was "a constitution
within" the wise man "founded in words," conceded that only "in
heaven, perhaps, a pattern of it is indeed laid up, for him that has
eyes to see, and seeing to settle himself therein. It matters nothing
whether it exists anywhere or shall exist."[16] It matters a great deal to
Langland, and perhaps in the restless yearning of his social vision

16. Plato, *Republic*, 9 (591e, 592), in *Great Dialogues of Plato*, tr. W. H. D.
Rouse (New York: Mentor Books, 1956), p. 393.

we can discern once again the image of God within man. For if the presence of the Kingdom of God, the mystical body of Christ, within our hearts compels us to try to give it a visible reality in the social world, perhaps in that effort we imitate the procession of Love in the Trinity which could not be satisfied "Til it hadde of þe erþe yeten hitselue."

The great human obstacle to the reformation of the world in man's image is cupidity. For a broad definition of this vice we can turn to Saint Augustine: "And so when a man lives according to man, not according to God, he is like the devil. . . . For it was God who said, 'I am the truth.' . . . But when a man lives according to himself . . . he certainly lives according to a lie."[17] Langland's personifications of the Deadly Sins are studies in cupidity in this extended sense. As human beings, they have chosen to define themselves by the sins whose names they bear, and, in living out their different lies, they feed on themselves in bitter loneliness. This loneliness has as much effect on us as their raffish humor. Most of the jokes in their scenes turn on failures of communication or on situations which isolate them.[18] Avarice, in his funniest lines, talks at cross purposes with Repentance because he does not know what "restitucion" means (B.V.230–36). Sloth simply falls asleep over the question of restitution (B.V.441). Gluttony's riotous camaraderie at Betty's alehouse gives way to isolation as the physical effects of overindulgence (graphically described) affront the senses of his companions and his family (B.V.296–362). Wrath stirs up discord in convents and monasteries because he has "no likyng . . . wiþ þo leodes to wonye" (B.V.176). This alienation operates at different levels of intensity throughout society; and, by its diversion of the human will into private, self-seeking, ultimately self-consuming activities, it blocks the emergence of the *corpus mysticum*. Several times in the poem society almost coalesces into its ideal form, only to have two or three self-seeking members turn away. In each case this foreshadows a general unraveling of the social fabric.

17. "Cum ergo vivit homo secundum hominem, non secundum Deum, similis est diabolo. . . . Deus est enim qui dixit, *Ego sum veritas* (Joan. XIV, 6). Cum vero vivit secundum se ipsum, hoc est secundum hominem, non secundum Deum, profecto secundum mendacium vivit." *De civitate Dei* 14.4.1, in *PL* 41:407.

18. Cf. Mary Carruthers, *The Search for Saint Truth: A Study of Meaning in* Piers Plowman (Evanston: Northwestern University Press, 1973), pp. 3–5.

The temptations that lead to this unraveling are most clearly represented by Lady Meed, one of Langland's finest creations. I do not think she is simply Cupidity, as Father Dunning says.[19] Her name means "reward," and, as frequently happens in Langland's best personifications, the moral ambiguities of the word are rendered by the ambiguities of the character. I agree with A. G. Mitchell who argues that she is amoral rather than immoral.[20] She hardly has the will power to embody a sin. Instead of showing the perverse self-determination which defines cupidity, Meed shows almost no self-determination at all. Marriage to False seems to her a jolly enough idea, but she would just as soon marry Conscience once the constant inducements of her former suitor and his entourage are removed. Her defense against Conscience's charges is not so much a plea for an evil principle as it is a reaction to a personal insult from a man proposed to her as a husband. Lady Meed is just a girl who can't say no, who is so stupefyingly alluring that she does not need to be positively evil to inspire evil thoughts in the heart of every man who looks at her. Her power comes simply from her complaisance.

A short speech by Theology gives a more abstract view of Lady Meed, but one that agrees with the dramatic ambiguity of her character. It also makes the identification with cupidity extremely difficult. Theology reproaches Civil for authorizing the marriage of Lady Meed to False "to wraþþe with truþe":

"For Mede is muliere of Amendes engendred
God graunted to gyue Mede to truþe,
And þow hast gyuen hire to a gilour, now god gyue þee sorwe!
The text telleþ þee noȝt so, Truþe woot þe soþe,
For *Dignus est operarius* his hire to haue,
And þow hast fest hire wiþ Fals; fy on þi lawe!

. . . .

Wel ye witen, wernardes, but if youre wit faille,
That Fals is feyntlees and fikel in his werkes,
And as a Bastard ybore of Belsabubbes kynne.
And Mede is muliere, a maiden of goode;
She myȝte kisse þe kyng for cosyn and she wolde."

(B.II.119–24, 129–33)

19. *A-Text*, p. 69.
20. *Lady Meed and the Art of Piers Plowman*, The 3rd Chambers Memorial Lecture (London: University of London, Athlone Press, 1956), esp. pp. 4–6.

Theology is no fool, and what he says should not be taken lightly. Later in the poem Study gives Theology her grudging approval: although it seems "mystier" and "derker" the deeper she looks into it and though "It is no Science forsoþe for to sotile Inne," still she loves it the better because "it leteþ best bi loue" (B.X.186–88, 190). Theology's present speech is dark and misty enough, certainly, and I suppose this is why critics have not subtled in it when discussing Lady Meed.[21] Theology pleads against the marriage of Meed to False because Meed's mother is Amends,[22] and God has promised to give Meed in marriage to Truth. It is hard to see how God could arrange such a marriage if Meed represented cupidity. Theology uses "truth" ambiguously, as Lady Holy Church did in the preceding Passus. When he blames Civil for arranging the wedding "to wraþe wiþ truþe," he is speaking of transcendent Truth, God Himself. When he says that God has promised "to gyue Mede to truþe," he is speaking of immanent truth, the presence of God in man guiding man to good works. If Meed were married to Truth she would appear in the world as the good reward of which Christ said, "dignus est operarius mercede sua."[23] Furthermore, her marriage to Truth would give her a share in Truth's ambiguity; her earthly meaning would gain a heavenly meaning as well. This is still somewhat dark and misty, and Langland's extended commentary on these ideas, the speech in which Conscience refuses to marry Meed, seems to have caused him some trouble.

The well-meaning king proposes to make an honest woman of Meed by marrying her to Conscience. Conscience refuses emphatically, saying that she corrupts the realm. Meed, outraged at this insult, defends herself with considerable skill, and claims (perhaps somewhat obscurely) that Conscience, not she, ruined the king's recent French campaign. She concludes, quite plausibly, that rewards are the king's inducements to loyal service, the hire of Church and labor, and the

21. Mitchell (p. 5) cites the passage in support of his theory that Lady Meed is ambiguous, but he does not discuss it in detail. John A. Yunk, in *The Lineage of Lady Meed: The Development of Mediaeval Venality Satire* (Notre Dame, Ind.: University of Notre Dame Press, 1963), p. 7, passes over the speech in two sentences of inaccurate paraphrase.

22. False is Meed's father as well as her would-be husband (B.II.25; C. III.121). Incest makes an interesting metaphor for cupidity, but I do not think Langland meant this. He seems to have jumbled up his personifications. The change of her father's name to "Fauel" in C.III.25 seems an effort to patch things up.

23. Luke 10:7. A.II.86 gives the full clause; C omits it.

medium of commerce. The king is convinced: "Quod þe kyng to Conscience, 'bi crist, as me þynkeþ, / Mede is worthi . . . þe maistrie to haue.'" (B.III.228–29). Conscience respectfully refutes the king with a careful, rather difficult differentiation of three terms: what we may call heavenly meed which "god of his grace gyueþ in his blisse / To hem that werchen wel while þei ben here" (232–33); "mesurelees" earthly meed which he equates with the bribes of Psalm 26:10 (Authorized Version); and "mesurable hire" (256), the just wage and just price which is not a meed at all. Both meeds have the quality of being measureless, rewards which bear no proportion to the works performed.[24] The equivocation which makes the same term yield meanings so emphatically opposed, *de bono* and *de malo*, symbolizes the peril of life in the field of folk between the two antithetical towers. The pursuit of a measureless reward in this world is a perverse imitation of the order of heaven and thus a commitment to hell.

A precedent for this kind of equivocation can be found in the Augustinian idea of cupidity by which man becomes his own end and thus a perverted image of God. Consider, for example, this analysis of earthly politics, with its pointed equivocation on "peace": "How much more is a man driven by the laws of his nature to enter into some sort of fellowship and, as far as possible, maintain peace with all men. After all, even wicked men fight for the peace of their own people, and would make all people their own if they could, so that all people and things might be subject to one and, bound to him, might yield themselves to his peace alone, whether for love or fear. For thus does pride perversely imitate God. It hates equality with fellow men under God. Rather it would impose its rule on its fellows, supplanting God. It hates God's just peace and loves its own wicked peace. Still, it cannot help loving peace of some sort. No vice is so utterly contrary to nature as to wipe out even its last traces."[25] Such an analysis, with its dismissal of all grand political designs as sinful expressions of

---

24. Cf. Lawlor, *Piers Plowman*, p. 29; Mitchell, *Lady Meed*, pp. 13–14.

25. "Quanto magis homo fertur quodammodo naturae suae legibus ad ineundam societatem pacemque cum hominibus, quantum in ipso est, omnibus obtinendam: cum etiam mali pro pace suorum belligerent, omnesque, si possint, suos facere velint, ut uni cuncti et cuncta deserviant; quo pacto, nisi in ejus pacem, vel amando, vel timendo consentiant? Sic enim superbia perverse imitatur Deum. Odit namque cum sociis aequalitatem sub illo: sed imponere vult sociis dominationem suam pro illo. Odit ergo justam pacem Dei et amat iniquam pacem suam: non amare tamen qualemcumque pacem nullo modo potest. Nullum quippe vitium ita contra naturam est, ut naturae deleat etiam extrema vestigia." *De civitate Dei* 19.12.2, in *PL* 41:639.

human pride, sets Dante's earthly paradise on its head. More to the
point here, though, is the fact that the play on "peace" which, in one
form or another, is a necessary goal of man, parallels exactly Langland's play on "mede," measureless reward.

As usual, Langland takes a position between Saint Augustine and
Dante. He introduces an intermediate term, measurable hire, to break
the fall from the first kind of meed to the second and give a Christian
significance to man's social and economic life in this world. He recog-
nizes and accepts Augustine's vision of human nature, and of the
perilous ambiguity of man's motives and powers which can save or
damn him, depending on whether or not they are in contact with
grace. This vision lies behind several equivocal personifications in the
poem and determines the topography of the opening scene. But Langland's concern throughout the poem always returns to that central
field of folk who live in a political community and on a money economy. His ambition, not shared by Augustine, is that this society be
reformed to the image of God, so that the Incarnation may be fulfilled in history. The question is, how? How can measurable hire reflect the infinite largesse of God and so transform man's economy into
an image of the heavenly economy?

The C-text gives evidence of how Langland struggled with this idea,
for Conscience's speech is revised extensively. First, the heavenly
meed is eliminated and the earthly, corrupt meed is opposed to measurable hire, which now has a new name, "mercede." This name
comes from the text in Theology's speech, "*dignus est operarius mercede sua,*" a quotation which disappears in the C version. He more
than makes up for this simplification, however, by adding an involved,
seventy-four-line conceit which is generally regarded as the ugly duck-
ling of the C revision.[26] Conscience compares the distinction between
meed and mercede to the distinction between the incorrect and correct grammatical relations of a substantive and an adjective in a sentence. The passage is hard to follow anyway, but it is entirely unintelligible if the reader forgets that meed and mercede are being

26. C.IV.355–409. For a short catalogue of critical abuse, see Donaldson,
C-Text, 79n. George Kane, in *Middle English Literature* (London: Methuen,
1951), says it "rivals Dante's account of the spots on the moon for sheer deliberate dullness" (p. 185). For a brief treatment of the medieval and ancient
background of this sort of grammatical metaphor, see Ernst Robert Curtius,
European Literature and the Latin Middle Ages, trans. Willard R. Trask (New
York: Harper and Row, 1953), pp. 414–16.

compared not to two *things* but to *relations* of things.[27] According to Conscience, "Relacioun rect," the relation that corresponds to mercede,

> "is a record of treuthe
> Folowynge and fyndynge out þe fundement of a strenghe
> And styfliche stande forth to strenghe þe fundement
> In kynde and in case and in þe cours of nombre.
> As a leel laborer byleueth with his maister
> In his pay and in his pite and in his puyr treuthe
> To pay hym yf he performe and haue pite yf he faileth
> And take hym for his trauaile al þat treuthe wolde."
>   (C.IV.346–53)[28]

So far this is clear enough. The right relation of substantive and adjective, with its agreement of kind (gender), number, and case, is a type of the right relation of laborer and master, with their strict proportion of work and reward for work. The laborer, whose type is the adjective, is naturally subordinate to the master, whose type is the substantive. Their relationship is governed by truth, and, as usual, this term complicates things. The line from laborer to master now appears to be a refraction of the line from man to God:

27. This point is missed by Margaret Amassian and James Sadowsky in an important article, "Mede and Mercede: A Study of the Grammatical Metaphor in 'Piers Plowman' C: IV: 335–409," *Neuphilologische Mitteilungen* 72 (1971): 457–76. After saying that the "two kinds of reward are being likened to two kinds of grammatical relationship" (463), they shift to a comparison of the rewards to the *terms* of a relationship: "Mede and Mercede are alike as substantive and adjective are alike in their inflectional agreement" (464). The difficulty of maintaining this alignment soon forces them to postulate "the fact that the poet is not saying what he means" (465; cf. 468). A complicating factor is their treatment of Langland's "direct and indirect relation" as referring to the link of relative pronoun to its antecedent, not to the grammatical agreement of adjective and noun. This is attractive in the light of a grammatical text they cite as an analogue (463n.), but not finally persuasive. It involves a double analogy (antecedent/relative and substantive/adjective) which keeps going out of focus; and it seems to counter the intent of C.IV.335–40, where the agreement of substantive and adjective (338) seems to be identical with the "relacions" (335–36), not an alternative to them.

28. Except where noted I am following the text as edited by Mitchell and included as an appendix in *Lady Meed*, pp. 26–27. This will eventually appear in the new edition of C being prepared by Mitchell and G. H. Russell for the Athlone Press of the University of London. I have omitted Mitchell's brackets and other editorial apparatus and supplied some punctuation.

"So of holy herte cometh hope and hardy relacioun,
Seketh and seweth his sustantif sauacioun
That is god the ground of al a graciouse antecedent.
And man is relatif rect yf he be rihte trewe.
He acordeth with crist in kynde *verbum caro factum est*
In case *credere in ecclesia* in holy kyrke to bileue
In nombre Rotye and aryse and remissioun to haue
Of oure sory synnes to be assoiled and yclansed
And lyue as oure crede vs kenneth with crist withouten ende.
This is relacion rect ryht as adiectyf and sustantyf
Acordeth in alle kyndes with his antecedent."

(C.IV.354–64)

The analogy is quite striking if one follows it carefully. Man in this world is like an adjective following and taking its form from its noun, his salvation. This is another way of expressing the operations of truth explained by Lady Holy Church. As immanent in man, truth projects man towards its transcendent aspect, "That is god the ground of al, a graciouse antecedent." God is antecedent of all the substantives under discussion here, so that man's social relationship to his master, which defines him in the world, is a figure of his relationship to his own salvation, which defines him in eternity. This does not arise simply from the nature of society. It is a mystery of grace, arising from the intersection of eternity and the temporal history that is society's medium when the Word was made flesh and man was made to accord "with crist in kynde." From this likeness in kind follow the likenesses of case and number. And the right ordering of the sentence which is this earthly life makes clear its reference to the divine Idea: it "Acordeth in alle kyndes with his antecedent."

The social structure of this "relacioun rect" is elaborated in the familiar form of king and commons:

"Ac relacioun rect is a ryhtful custume
As a kyng to clayme the comune at his wille
To folowe and to fynde hym and fecche at hem his consayl
That here loue to his lawe Thorw al þe lond acorde.
So comune claymeth of a kyng thre kyne thynges,
Lawe, loue, and lewete, and hym lord antecedent,
Bothe heued and here kyng haldyng with no parteyȝe

Bote standynge as a stake þat stiketh in a mere
Bytwene two lordes for a trewe marke."

$$(C.IV.376-84)^{29}$$

Here "Lawe, loue, and lewete" are the equivalents in the earthly
kingdom of the kind, case, and number that bind man to the heavenly
kingdom; and the king as antecedent is the earthly type of the divine
Idea. Law in the kingdom is the matrix of love, which makes it
accord "Thorw al þe lond." "Lewete" or "leute"—which is "exact
justice; strict adherence to the letter of the law"[30]—is thus a discipline
of social love in each citizen. We shall have occasion to return to this
alliterative triad which, as P. M. Kean points out, recur in the poem
"with almost the persistence of 'Dowel, Dobet, and Dobest the thridde'
in the *Vita*."[31]

This more elaborate order in the kingdom is once again refracted
through the Incarnation into the bond between man and God:

"Ac adiectyf and sustantyf is as y her tolde,
That is vnite, acordaunce in case, in gendre, and in noumbre,
And is to mene in oure mouth more ne mynne
But þat alle maner men, wymmen, and childrene
Sholde confourme hem to o kynde, on holy kyrke to bileue,
And coueyte þe case when thei couthe vnderstande
To syke for here synnes and soffre harde penaunces."

$$(C.IV.396-402)$$

29. Skeat has a line just preceding this passage which Mitchell omits, so
that in this and subsequent passages Skeat's line numbers are higher by one.

30. So defined by Donaldson, *C-Text*, 66 n.4. P. M. Kean, in "Love, Law,
and Lewte in *Piers Plowman*," *Review of English Studies* 15 (1964):254–57,
rejects this definition, but the one she offers instead is not really much different. She adduces several supporting texts from Aristotle and St. Thomas
which are quite well chosen and relevant, but which could illustrate Donaldson's definition just as easily. Her discomfort with Donaldson's definition can,
I think, be compared with the discomfort of some critics over the usual gloss
of "kynde knowyng" as "natural knowledge." Both glosses seem too dry and
uninteresting to be connected in such an immediate way with love. But their
affective content in *Piers Plowman* seems peculiar to Langland and probably
cannot find clear corroboration in external philological evidence. Amassian and
Sadowsky make the good suggestion that for Langland "leute" combines the
senses of *fidelitas* and *fides*, especially in conjunction with the similarly ambiguous "treuthe" (pp. 461–62, 471–72).

31. "Love, Law, and Lewte," p. 241.

At this point we should note a shift in terms. Earlier in the passage
the man who was "rihte trewe" accorded with Christ "in kynde"
through the Incarnation, "in case" through belief in the Church, and
"in nombre" through the promise of resurrection and remission of
sins after death. Now Conscience tells us that true men in society
accord *with each other* in "o kynde"; they aspire to a natural state of
sorrow and penance for sin which will agree *in case* with the suffering
Christ because He willingly took on man's *number*, mortality and
the capacity for suffering. They

> "soffre harde penaunces
> For þat ilke lordes loue þat for oure loue deyede
> And coueytede oure kynde and be kald in oure name
> *Deus homo*
> And nyme hym in to oure noumbre now and euere more
> *Qui in caritate manet in deo manet et deus in eo.*
> Thus is man and mankynde in maner of a sustantyf
> As *hic et hec homo* askyng an adiectyf
> Of thre trewe termisones *trinitas vnus deus*
> *Nominatiuo pater et filius et spiritus sanctus.*"
>
> (C.IV.402–9)

The final shift in terms is the most fundamental and daring. Man,
who was once adjective to God's substantive, is now substantive to
God's adjective. The normal doctrinal description of Christ as *Deus
homo* is analyzed grammatically to ratify man's finite image of the
infinite God. Langland grounds this image in the Incarnation and
evolves it socially. Man's agreement in kind with Christ is made
manifest in the world through his agreement in kind with other men.
Love, law, and leute define the social aspect of charity, and, according to Saint John's epistle (4:16): "*Qui in caritate manet in deo
manet et deus in eo.*" The man true in society is "a god by þe gospel
a grounde and o lofte."

All of this began as a definition of mercede as opposed to meed,
although the reader may be forgiven if this has slipped his mind. The
point is that just as the infinite God finds His proper image in finite
man, so His infinite rewards find their proper image in man's finite
rewards. Mercede, measurable hire, is the only true reflection of
God's immeasurable meed. To return to Theology's terms in the B-
text, only by marriage to Truth could Meed be made an honest
woman. Thus Theology was right in defending her, but Conscience

was also right in rejecting her. Lady Meed is not presently married to Truth, so, by the sort of judgment proper to Conscience, she is a concrete evil.

Because God submitted to the rigors of finitude in the Incarnation, the finite justice of man's dealings with his fellow man can be in some sense deified. But measureless meed on earth "perversely imitates God." It is the indirect relation which turns awry the sentence of life:

> "Indirect thyng is as ho so coueytede
> Alle kyn kynde to knowe and to folowe
> And withoute [case] to cache to and come to bothe nombres
> In whiche ben gode and nat gode and graunte here neyþer wille.
> . . . .
> So indirect is inlyche to coueyte
> To acorde in alle kynde and in alle kyn nombre
> Withouten coest and care and alle kyn trauayle."
>   (C.IV.365–68, 373–75)[32]

The man seeking an unlimited good in this life is separating himself from the divine order. He is trying to be a god and immortal and thus attain to the kind and number of God, without guiding himself by the teachings of the Church and matching the divine Substantive in case. This deviation has social consequences as well:

> "Ac þe moste partie of the peple now puyr indirect semeth
> For they wilnen and wolden as beste were for hemsulue
> Thow the kyng and þe comune al þe coest hadde.
> Such inparfit peple repreueth alle resoun
> And halt hem vnstedefast for hem lakketh case.
> As relatifs indirect reccheth thei neuere
> Of the cours of case so thei cacche suluer,
> Be the peccunie ypaied thow parties chyde.

---

32. In line 367 I have departed from Mitchell's text to retain Skeat's "case." Mitchell substitutes "cause," which has the authority of better MSS. I think "case" is preferable because of the presence of "kynde" and "noumbres" nearby. For a scribe who was not following Langland's conceit carefully, "cause" would be a likely substitution since it makes the line stand on its own intelligibly; "case" is therefore a *durior lectio* and, as such, a better candidate for authenticity. Cf. the passage cited next, where "case" is used in such a way as to complete the meaning of this passage.

He þat mede may lacche maketh lytel tale,
Nyme he a noumbre of nobles or of shillynges.
How þat cliauntes acorde acounteth mede litel."

(C.IV.385–95)

Here in a nutshell is the whole social malaise of Langland's England. The desire for money causes people to "halt hem vnstedefast." The friars are the prime example of this. Following an exaggerated doctrine of poverty, they have no stable home or endowment. Their total want is only too easily turned into total rapacity. They wax "out of noumbre" and preach "That alle þynges vnder heuene ouȝte to ben in comune" (B.XX.269, 276),[33] thus threatening to abolish the whole social grammar by which man is led back to "god the ground of al, a graciouse antecedent." The wandering friars are more popular confessors than the parish priests; so a rivalry breaks out within the clergy. Parish priests complain that they can no longer make a decent living from their depleted rural churches; so they, too, become wanderers, going off to London to earn easy fees saying Mass for the rich (B.Prol.83–98). The parish system is thus cut loose from its moorings. Laymen and religious pick up the infection and practice the spurious devotion of pilgrimages. The typical pilgrim has been to dozens of shrines and has souvenirs to prove it, but he has never heard of the shrine of Truth (B.V.515–36). Pardoners and other emissaries of Rome move in to fleece the faithful, then transport currency illegally out of England (B.Prol.68–82; IV.128–33). Wandering of one sort or another is a symbol of the radical unintelligibility of contemporary society, and the man searching society for his own image and the image of God is himself reduced to restless, aimless wandering, and to the uneasy consciousness of embodying to some extent the very evils he criticizes in society.[34]

All these problems exemplify the lack of love, law, and leute, those qualities which recur so often in Langland's vision of an ideal society. At several points in the poem they have almost a sacred character, and this probably reflects the late medieval tendency to mix legality and liturgy. Lawyers described themselves as priests at the altar of law, and nearly turned *lex* and *iustitia*—compare law and leute—into

33. On the friars' numberlessness see Bloomfield, *Apocalypse*, p. 145; on a parallel to this idea in monastic thought see pp. 47–50.
34. This uncomfortable self-consciousness is most clearly expressed in C. VI.1–108, but it also pervades the whole poem in each of the three versions. Kirk, *Dream Thought*, passim, gives particular emphasis to this aspect of the poem.

sacraments.[35] So we have Lady Holy Church complaining that Lady Meed has "ylakked my lemman þat leautee is hoten" (B.II.21), and Trajan's proud claim that "al þe clergie vnder crist ne myȝte me cracche fro helle,/ But oonliche loue and leautee and my laweful domes" (B.XI.144–45). Lady Holy Church uses two of the terms and, perhaps, implies the third as she links the social order of heaven and earth, just after describing Love's Incarnation:

> "Forþi is loue ledere of þe lordes folk of heuene
> And a meene, as þe Mair is, bitwene þe commune & þe kyng;
> Right so is loue a ledere and þe lawe shapeþ;
> Vpon man for hise mysdedes þe mercyment he taxeþ.
> And for to knowen it kyndely, it comseþ by myght,
> And in þe herte þere is the heed and þe heiȝe welle."
>
> (B.I.159–64)

And, in the C-text, as we saw earlier, the ideal society whose image wells up in the redeemed human heart will provide for all men "Yf loue and leaute and owre lawe be trewe" (C.VIII.260).

Conscience's speech before the king, in which he rejects Meed and predicts the coming of "oon cristene kyng," contains a particularly beautiful vision of that ideal society brought forth into the world. In it he sets up an odd opposition among the three terms:

> Shal na moore Mede be maister on erþe,
> Ac loue and lowenesse and leautee togideres;
> Thise shul ben Maistres on moolde trewe men to saue.
> And whoso trespaseþ to truþe or takeþ ayein his wille,
> Leaute shal don hym lawe and no lif ellis.
> Shal no sergeant for þat seruice were a silk howue,
> Ne no pelure in his panelon for pledynge at þe barre;
> Mede of mysdoeres makeþ manye lordes,
> And ouer lordes lawes ledeþ þe Reaumes.
> Ac kynde loue shal come ȝit and Conscience togideres
> And make of lawe a laborer; swich loue shal arise
> And swich pees among þe peple and a parfit truþe
> That Iewes shul wene in hire wit, and wexen glade,
> That Moyses or Messie be come into myddelerþe,
> And haue wonder in hire hertes þat men beþ so trewe.
>
> (B.III.290–304)

35. See Kantorowicz, pp. 93–94, 115–19, 141–42.

The triad is first altered: "lowenesse" replaces "lawe." Then "Leaute," personified, becomes a judge administering law instead of the subjects' disposition to obey the law. Finally, "kynde loue" will come with Conscience and reduce law to an obedient subject laboring in the field, as men do now in obedience to the law. In a subsequent passage, Reason is more circumstantial and humbling in his allocation of tasks:

> "And if þow werche it in werk I wedde myne eris
> That lawe shal ben a laborer and lede afeld donge,
> And loue shal lede þi lond as þe leef lykeþ!"
>
> (B.IV.146–48)

And so it seems that when the world is reformed to man's image and God's, two of the recurring triad will turn on the third and render him subject.

Is Langland preaching anarchy? In what sense can leute, a strict regard for the law, become instead the norm of law? The answer to the first question, of course, is no, and the answer to the second leads us into a consideration of the curiously comic tone of Langland's apocalyptic vision. Law, as I said earlier, is the matrix of love in society. Yet as law achieves objective form in the world, as positive written law, it becomes liable to exploitation by selfish men. Langland's king rebukes Law for this; or, looking through the personification, he blames his crooked lawyers who have been "overmastered" by Meed (B.IV.174–81). Law becomes one of those equivocal terms that can be good or evil depending on whether they follow God's truth or man's lie. Leute, a human disposition, is not similarly equivocal. If its outer manifestation is obedience to the law, its inner impulse is love. It is the social expression of the Love that came down to alloy itself with earth. Written laws in the world, with their tendency to legalism in the pejorative sense, are a response to the lawless tendencies of fallen man. When society is redeemed, this sort of law will be unnecessary, since men will be guided by an inner impulse toward harmony, that is, by leute. It will be as if all society were to move to the music that rose when Christ harrowed hell, freeing men from an earlier Law, and bringing the four daughters of God together in a dance (B.XVIII.424–25).

We have noted in chapter 2 that Langland tends, almost in spite of himself, to glorify minstrels and lunatics and fools. In each revision, this was a cause of discomfort to him because he knew that most of these people in the real world were scoundrels and loafers. In the C-text, many of the references are cut or turned against the minstrels. But C introduces some new figures, the "lunatik lollers" (C.X.107) who wander "witlees" just as "Peter dude and Paul" (C.X.111–12). They have the gift of prophecy, and are

> murye-mouthede men, mynstrales of heuene,
> And godes boyes, bordiours, as the bok telleth,
> *Si quis uidetur sapiens, fiet stultus ut sit sapiens.*
> (C.X.126–27)[36]

In the end of the poem, the only men who stand by Conscience and go into the besieged barn of Unity are these same happy-go-lucky types. All others side with Antichrist:

> And al þe Couent cam to welcome a tyraunt
> And alle hise as wel as hym, saue oonly fooles;
> Which foolis were wel gladdere to deye
> Than to lyue lenger siþ Leute was so rebuked.
> (B.XX.60–63)[37]

The class in society which seems least amenable to law is the only one to rally to the defense of leute. What appears in this world as a strict regard for law is, *sub specie aeternitatis*, the "fre liberal wille" of God's minstrels. It is the strict regard for the measure of the dance that sets free the movements of the dancer.

In the last two Passūs of *Piers Plowman* there is a pervasive sense of *déjà vu*. There are echoes of words and situations from the beginning of the poem, and their cumulative effect is to damp the exuberance of Passus XVIII and prepare the reader for the collapse of the holy society established by Grace. Much of the time Will is a passive on-looker, as he was in the *Visio*. Again and again the reader is reminded that he has been here before, that this enterprise begun with such high hopes is doomed.

36. The Latin text is 1 Cor. 3:18. Donaldson (*C-Text*, pp. 144–47) connects this passage with the Franciscan idea of *Joculatores Domini*.
37. Cf. C.XXIII.60–63.

A social idealist like Langland, or like his dreamer, always faces a world that is churlishly unresponsive to his redeemed vision of it. The dream is right, and yet the waking world gives it the lie and always seems to win the argument. In Langland's case the dream has a rightness grounded on an objective historical fact, the Redemption, and this only makes more heartbreaking its wreckage when he sends it forth into the real world it was meant to transform. To give equal recognition to the validity and the perishability of his vision, as he does in the conclusion of his poem, is an act of rare imaginative courage.

Throughout his life the dreamer has pondered his vision of a redeemed society, tracing it through all his inner faculties to the source of their redemption in history, the Incarnation. Society's salvation must be as sure as his own, for their source is the same. Having reached that central event in history, the dreamer can recast the trials of his hypothetical kingdom in their most fundamental terms: at bottom the struggle is between the kingdom of Grace and Antichrist.[38] Now when Piers goes into the field the "literal" grains he sows have become "spiritually" the cardinal virtues. His four oxen are now the four Evangelists. His four bullocks are the Fathers of the Church who harrow the crops of "holy scripture" with "an olde and a newe" harrow, "*Id est, vetus testamentum et nouum*" (B.XIX.262–311). The half-acre of the *Visio* has been allegorized, and this to the Christian Middle Ages means that it has been reconstituted in terms of its deepest reality.

This terminology suggests the famous tradition of the allegorical reading of Scripture, or, more precisely, the fourfold sense of Scripture. I should like to suggest, tentatively, a relationship between this tradition and the structure of Langland's poem after the Pardon scene, a relationship which may shed particular light on the poem's conclusion. As is well known, medieval exegetes distinguished two kinds of meaning in the Bible, literal (or historical) and spiritual. The first had reference to the reality of words and things in the Bible, the second to their significance, revealed to the prayerful reader by the Holy

---

38. In so conceiving the theme of the last two Passūs, I am departing from Morton Bloomfield's analysis (*Apocalypse*, pp. 114, 125), at least insofar as it seems to imply Langland's belief in the imminent end of the world. As a general rule, I think it would be safer to say that the role of such millenarianism in *Piers Plowman* is somewhat like that of Platonic reminiscence in Wordsworth's "Ode: Intimations of Immortality." In each case the poetic *use* of a belief is more important than—and does not imply—actual adherence to the belief.

Spirit. The second sort of meaning had three divisions: the allegorical, by which the literal meaning was a figure of the Incarnation and Redemption; the tropological, by which the literal meaning revealed the right ordering of our lives in love (*caritas*); and the anagogical, by which the literal meaning revealed the union with God of the individual soul at the end of life (a union which could have a transitory anticipation in mystical contemplation), or the union of all faithful souls with God at the end of time. Some commentators varied the order of these meanings, having tropology emerge first from the literal sense, followed by allegory.[39] Theologians commonly projected these four senses onto history and other aspects of created reality.[40] One such projection was the doctrine of the "triple coming of Christ," discussed in some detail by Père de Lubac, and given in convenient summary by the twelfth-century commentator Henry of Marcy: "But according to the spiritual sense all that Scripture of the Old Testament spreads itself out in the past with a foresight of the future, foretelling a triple coming of Christ, whether it be the first, which was secret and lowly and behind us in time; or the second, present each day, which is felt, inward and sweet, by holy men; or the third, which is awaited, terrible and plain to all, at the end of time."[41] Each of these comings of Christ was aligned with one of the three spiritual senses of Scripture. The first corresponded to the allegorical sense because it was that actual Incarnation of the Godhead which all the Old Testament had prefigured. The second corresponded to the tropological sense because it was the motivation of the heart to good works which was the continuing presence of the Incarnation in subsequent history. The third corresponded to the anagogical sense because it was the moment of final reunion of all the souls of the just with God, the moment when

39. There were other variations which took anagogy from the last place, but the two I have mentioned are the dominant orders. Henri de Lubac discusses the significance of these different orders in *Exégèse Médiévale*, 4 vols. (Paris: Aubier, 1959), 1:144–69, 191–98.

40. A good example is Saint Bonaventure's *De Reductione Artium ad Theologum*, which applied the four senses to the liberal and mechanical arts. See *Opera Omnia* 5 (Quaracchi, 1891), and the Latin-English edition of Sister Emma Thérèse Healy (St. Bonaventure, N.Y.: St. Bonaventure College, 1939).

41. "Secundum sensum vero spiritualem, tota ipsa Scriptura Veteris Testamenti futura prospiciens in anteriora se extendit, triplicem Christi praenuntians adventum; vel primum, qui occultus fuit et humilis, et jam nobis est praeteritus; vel secundum, qui praesens quotidie a sanctis intimus sentitur et dulcis; vel tertium, qui manifestus et terribilis in fine temporum exspectatur." *Tractatus de peregrinante civitate Dei* 1, in *PL* 204:259c; cited (with a misprint: "proscipiens" for "prospiciens") by Père de Lubac in *Exégèse Médiévale*, 2:621, n.4.

Christ was once more to be externally present in the world, as its judge.

Now such a three-part division of history as this may well have been Langland's point of departure in dividing the greater part of his poem into a *Vita de Dowel, Vita de Dobet*, and *Vita de Dobest*. It at least forms a helpful frame of reference for the discussion of this structural problem. Important features of this scheme are that it involves no mystical withdrawal from the world, and that in its anagogical term, the third coming of Christ, it has distinctly social, even political, implications. The reunion of all the faithful with God must involve some consideration of the way men unite with one another in social institutions.

Since the *Vita de Dowel* is clearly concerned with the right ordering of our lives in love, we might conclude that Langland is closer to those theologians who place the tropological before the allegorical sense, in their emergence from the literal. This position is defensible, but, since Langland's relationship to his intellectual background is always indirect and idiosyncratic, we might test this proposition more closely. Again and again in *Piers Plowman* our will's movement toward good works is seen to imply or even to reenact the central events of sacred history, the Incarnation and the Redemption. Lady Holy Church tells us that the heart's tendency toward good works is the counterpart of God's overflowing Love (which is His Son) coming down to alloy Himself with earth. When the soul resists the temptations of the devil, Piers takes up the second stake of the Trinity, which was there waiting for him, and humanity is joined to Godhead. What is implied or reenacted in each of these events must precede them, both logically and chronologically. The progress through "Dowel" to the vision of the Redemption in "Dobet" is, as I suggested earlier, a tracing back of Langland's vision of individual and social goodness to its source and premise in the Redemption. A theologian like Saint Bonaventure might call it a *reductio* of tropology to allegory. So the logical order of the three terms in Langland's mind seems to place allegory before tropology, even though the form of his poem reverses them.

The *reductio* can be analyzed in terms of Piers's roles in Passus XVI and Passus XVIII of the B-text. In the first, which completes the transition from "Dowel" to "Dobet," Piers is seen within man, making the decisive move in defense of the Tree of Charity against the attacks of the Devil. This is the realm of tropology, of the right ordering of life helped by the grace of the Redemption. This scene suddenly falls away to reveal the realm of allegory, the life of Christ; and when we next see Piers in Passus XVIII he is Christ's human nature. Passus XIX opens with a vision of the wounded Christ, who still looks like Piers to Will:

> "Is þis Iesus þe Iustere," quod I, "þat Iewes dide to deþe?
> Or is it Piers þe Plowman? who peynted hym so rede?"
> Quod Conscience and kneled þo, "þise arn Piers armes,
> Hise colours and his cote Armure; ac he þat comeþ so blody
> Is crist wiþ his cros, conquerour of cristene."
>
> (B.XIX.10–14)

Conscience then launches into yet another narration of Christ's life, upon the pretext of Will's confusion about the names "Christ" and "Jesus." Among other things Conscience points out the ultimate unity of allegory and tropology in the person of Christ. In His life Christ "did well" and "did better," and after His resurrection He taught "dobest":

> In his Iuuentee þis Iesus at Iewene feeste
> Water into wyn turnede, as holy writ telleþ.
> And þere bigan god of his grace to do wel:
> For wyn is likned to lawe and lif holynesse,
>
> . . . .
>
> And whan he was woxen moore, in his moder absence,
> He made lame to lepe and yaf light to blynde
> And fedde wiþ two fisshes and with fyue loues
> Sore afyngred folk, mo þan fyue þousand.
> Thus he confortede carefulle and caughte a gretter name
> The which was dobet, where þat he wente.
> [There follows an account of His death and resurrection and appearances to the apostles.]
> And whan þis dede was doon do best he þouȝte,
> And yaf Piers pardon, and power he grauntede hym,
> Myght men to assoille of alle manere synnes,
> To alle maner men mercy and forȝifnesse. . .
>
> (B.XIX.108–11, 124–29, 182–85)

The moral qualities in us gain their full meaning, as Do-well, Do-better, and Do-best, from their previous embodiment in Christ, who fought in Piers's arms, *humana natura*. This is the *reductio* or tracing back of tropology to allegory. In Christ we see the synthesis of our subjective moral life and the objective center of past history.

There is another such synthesis, implied by this first one, with its historical or objective term in the future. It will be found in the return of Christ to the stage of history at the end of time. This is the realm of anagogy, admirably described by Père de Lubac: "L'anagogie réalise donc la perfection et de l'allégorie et de la tropologie, en achevant leur synthèse. Elle n'est ni 'objective', comme la première, ni 'subjective', comme la seconde. Au-delà de cette division, elle réalise leur unité. Elle intègre le sens total et définitif. Elle vise, dans l'éternité, la fusion du mystère et de la mystique. Autrement dit, la réalité eschatologique atteinte par l'anagogie est la réalité éternelle, en laquelle toute autre a sa consommation. Elle est dans son état définitif ce 'testamentum novum, quod est regnum caelorum'. Elle constitue 'la Plénitude du Christ.' "[42] If we recall the discussion of the public, corporate role of Conscience, Reason, and other faculties we would normally consider subjective, we can see a distinct resemblance to Père de Lubac's description of anagogy. The synthesis of subjective and objective which we see in a figure like Conscience counseling the king on the public stage of history is attended by eschatological imagery in his speech on the perfect society. Eschatology and anagogy are the dominant modes of the last two Passūs where Langland once again builds that society, now in terms which show most explicitly its divine inspiration. Moral or tropological realities, properly subjective, are brought out into the light of historical day. Piers's grain and his plow and his oxen are now virtues and promptings of grace. History, in this anagogic light, is foreshortened, once again reduced to its image, somewhat as it is in the pageant witnessed by Dante in the Earthly Paradise.[43] We witness the founding of the Church, its corruption, and the disasters that will precede the Second Coming passing by us with the speed and transparent significance of thought—of thought "objectified."

42. *Exégèse Médiévale*, 2:632–33.
43. *Purgatorio* 32. See Charles S. Singleton's discussion of the representation of history in this canto in *Dante Studies, I: Commedia, Elements of Structure* (Cambridge: Harvard University Press, 1965), pp. 45–60.

There are several subtle touches in this narrative; for instance, the ease with which Piers slides from his identity with Christ to his identity with Peter. The sacramental relationship between Christ and His vicar is nicely rendered by giving them the same visible *humana natura*. When Piers and Grace establish the institutional Church we hear him speak in familiar tones:

> "Ayeins þi greynes," quod Grace, "bigynneþ for to ripe,
> Ordeigne þee an hous, Piers, to herberwe Inne þi cornes."
> "By god! Grace," quod Piers, "ye moten gyue tymber,
> And ordeyne þat hous er ye hennes wende."
> And Grace gaf hym þe cros, wiþ þe garland of þornes,
> That crist vpon Caluarie for mankynde on pyned.
> And of his baptisme and blood þat he bledde on roode
> He made a manere morter, and mercy it highte.
> And þerwiþ Grace bigan to make a good foundement,
> And watlede it and walled it wiþ hise peynes and his passion;
> And of al holy writ he made a roof after;
> And called þat hous vnitee, holy chirche on englissh.
>
> (B.XIX.317–28)

When Piers speaks with such rough practicality to Grace we recognize the hurried, efficient foreman of the half-acre. We recognize, too, for the first time, that these tones are perfectly appropriate to the bluff, impulsive fisherman of the Gospels. The practical tone of Piers's request is carried through the building of Unity in a particularly sharp illustration of Langland's technique in writing explicit allegory. The gifts of grace are perfectly balanced—half-line for half-line—with the concrete details of the building trade. Mercy is a mortar; Grace is a "foundement"; Holy Writ is a roof; and Christ's pains and passions wattle and wall the barn. And, in the synthetic, anagogic manner of this last part of the poem, the sign and the thing signified are equally present to us.

This new dimension is also seen in those episodes which most clearly recall early episodes in the poem. When Grace gives "ech man a grace to gide wiþ hymseluen" (B.XIX.227), following Saint Paul on the "divisions of grace" (1 Cor. 12:4), we are witnessing again Piers's assignment of tasks on the half-acre (B.VI.3ff.). When Conscience calls in Kind with his pestilences and his lieutenants "Deeþ" and "Elde," and then relents out of pity (B.XX.76–108), we recall

Piers's dealings with Hunger (B.VI.171–80, 199–201). We might call the early scenes, and even the whole *Visio*, the "literal" or historical portion of *Piers Plowman*. Scenes like those we have mentioned in the *Visio* are full of implicit meaning which becomes explicit in their reenactment in the *Vita de Dobest*. In both places they are presentations of social, historical reality, but in the second this reality is shot through with a higher meaning as time touches that eternity which is its consummation. This coming together of anagogy and history after the fusion of the two levels of meaning—allegory and tropology—that lie between them is the eschatological reality of which Père de Lubac speaks.

Why, then, does the poem not end in triumph? Even without reference to anagogy and similar concepts, the reader might expect this of a last section called *Vita de Dobest*. To answer this question we must return to what we said early in the chapter about the disparity between the logic of Langland's social vision and its emotional aspirations. When Langland spoke of the perfection of society and the emergence as corporate entities of the best qualities of individual men, he did so in the terms of a popular political philosophy which had conferred a new value upon the world and its institutions. The prominent role played by a new, ultimate king shows the secular character of his ideal, just as it does in Dante. He is more traditional than Dante, however, in tracing this ideal back not to Rome, but to Christ. This is particularly clear in the grammatical analogy of Conscience, where the Incarnation is the nexus of the political and divine orders. Langland cannot finally envision the perfection of the secular order in any other way than in its end. For him there is no earthly paradise. The Earthly City must yield to the City of God. Saint Augustine, viewing from afar the collapse of the Roman Empire, could contemplate this truth with equanimity. Langland, in the midst of a collapsing society in whose old ideals he believed passionately, can contemplate it only with dismay and pain. In the centuries since Augustine wrote, human society had given itself a new rationale, a new way of judging itself on its own terms. If the judgment was harsh, as Langland's was, it was still, for a man like him, a judgment which issued in a zeal for reform of the secular order, not a mystic's contemptuous dismissal of it.[44] So when time and time's creatures must pass away before the

44. On this shift in the attitude toward the world and its reflection in Middle English literature, see Donald Howard, *The Three Temptations* (Princeton: Princeton University Press, 1965).

glory of the returning Savior, the sense of triumph could well be hard
to sustain. After all, the only secular manifestations of the Second
Coming are pestilence, destruction, the failure of Life, and the
scourges of Kind.

When forced to the bitter conclusion of his divided attitude toward
the world, Langland does not evade it. Instead, he dramatizes it in
the most marvelous way. The army of Kind is called in to help Conscience, and, as it pursues Life, proves to be distressingly indifferent
to obstacles in its path:

> And Elde after hym; and ouer myn heed yede
> And made me balled bifore and bare on þe croune;
> So harde he yede ouer myn heed it wole be sene euere.
> "Sire yuele ytauȝt Elde!" quod I, "vnhende go wiþ þe!
> Siþ whanne was þe wey ouer mennes heddes?
> Haddestow be hende," quod I, "þow woldest haue asked leeue."
> "Ye, leue, lurdeyn?" quod he, and leyde on me wiþ Age,
> And hitte me vnder þe ere; vnneþe may ich here.
> He buffetted me aboute þe mouþ and bette out my wangteeþ;
> And gyued me in goutes: I may noȝt goon at large.
> And of þe wo þat I was Inne my wif hadde ruþe
> And wisshed ful witterly þat I were in heuene.
> For þe lyme þat she loued me fore and leef was to feele
> On nyghtes namely, whan we naked weere,
> I ne myghte in no manere maken it at hir wille,
> So Elde and heo hadden it forbeten.
> And as I seet in þis sorwe I sauȝ how kynde passede
> And deeþ drogh neiȝ me; for drede gan I quake,
> And cryde to kynde: "out of care me brynge!"
>
> (B.XX.183–201)

The passage is funny, pathetic, and chilling at the same time. To
grasp its difficult irony is to grasp the complexity of Langland's attitude toward the world. When the dreamer is struck by Kind's lieu-
tenant, who has been called in to fight Antichrist, his response, in
effect, is, "Say, what is this? I'm on *your* side!" There is no question
of rising to the superiority of *contemptus mundi*. He is too intimately
involved in this collapse. As Bloomfield points out, "the attacks of
Antichrist upon the Church are a kind of correlative to the progress

of death within him,"[45] and, we might add, so are the counterattacks of Kind's army. The last fruition of the Incarnation in history seems to be the destruction of the very world on which it conferred so intense a value. The last fruits of Will's unflinching search for the home of Do-well in the world seem to be the humiliations of old age and the awful presence of death.

When Unity collapses, Conscience must leave it and become once again a pilgrim. The stable order in which he can come forth in his corporate aspect has dissolved, and he must once more retreat to his individual, internal aspect. His departure from Unity is his return to the individual heart of Will the dreamer, and at the same time, the return of Will to consciousness: "And siþþe he gradde after Grace til I gan awake" (B.XX.386). The two of them will finish their search together, with their goal the same, but its shape unknown. One might even surmise that in that uncertainty there is an element of relief.

45. *Apocalypse*, p. 16.

4. Learning and Grace

CERTAINLY the most confused portion of *Piers Plowman* is the *Vita de Dowel*, in which Will makes his progress through a succession of internal faculties to that innermost point where he confronts Anima and witnesses the Redemption. Langland was brought to a standstill in this section. The A-text breaks off inconclusively in Passus XI (i.e., B.X). The B-text resumes after a lapse of some years and pushes on to *Dobet*, but still must undergo extensive revision in the C-text. Even the final version is marred by wild digressions and a remaining confusion of purpose.

The issues that cause all this trouble are, mainly, those of the life of the intellect and its relation to man's salvation. Langland's age was characterized by a tendency to distinguish sharply between learning and the more obviously religious aspects of spiritual life, denying to the first a direct relevance to salvation and imbuing the second with an emotional mysticism. This distinction is entertained in Langland's poem but it is specifically rejected in the speech of Imaginatif in Passus XII. Because Langland does try to maintain the connection between the two kinds of interior life and give a spiritual value to learning, the background of his thought is more likely to be found in treatises on learning such as *The Didascalicon* of Hugh of Saint Victor, *De Reductione Artium* of Saint Bonaventure, and the allegorical *Anticlaudian* of Alain de Lille, than in the more single-minded mysticism of Walter Hilton's *Scale of Perfection* or *The Cloud of Unknowing*.

Langland's most general complaint against the men of learning in his own time is that they sell their talents for personal profit. Why this is wrong Langland explains in an odd listing of the four elements:

Ac to bugge water ne wynd ne wit ne fir þe ferþe,
Thise foure þe fader of heuene made to þis foold in commune;
Thise ben truþes tresores trewe folk to helpe,
That neuere shul wexe ne wanye wiþouten god hymselue.

(B.VII.53–56)

In C he develops these lines into a more specific condemnation of the sin:

For hit is symonye, to sulle that send is of grace;
That is, witt and water, wynd, and fuyr the furthe,
These foure sholden be fre to alle folk that hit nedeth.

(C.X.55–57)

The mention of simony and grace recalls C's modification of the passage on Sir Inwit. C called Inwit "godes owen good, hus grace and hus tresoure" where B had been more careful, placing Inwit "after þe grace of god" (C.XI.175; B.IX.60). We might also recall B's description of speech, which is wit's expression, as the "spire . . . of grace / And goddes gleman and a game of heuene" (B.IX.103–4). To sell speech or wit is to bind what should be a type or symbol of the infinite to a finite, unworthy end. It is to hinder the free exuberance of God playing through His creation. It is, in fact, something like the desecration of a sacrament. One of the leading reproaches against Lady Meed is that "Clergie and coueitise she coupleþ togidres" (B.III.165). The results of this unholy marriage are best exemplified in the gluttonous friar-master of Passus XIII.

There is another, subtler kind of "coueitise" that can be associated with learning. This is the coueitise of learning itself, for its own sake, forgetting its status as a means of reaching God, or, more precisely, as a symbolic imitation and invocation of divine Wisdom. Here, as elsewhere, we are tempted to live by man's lie rather than God's truth. This is the fault Study and Anima both refer to when they warn the dreamer "*non plus sapere quam oportet sapere*" (B.X.121; B.XV.69; cf. Rom. 12:3). The counsel not to try to know more than we should, though, carries with it its own temptation; for we can misinterpret it to urge a contempt for learning. Will succumbs to this in his outbursts of anti-intellectualism in Passūs X and XI. The difficult point to remember is that the counsel of Study and Anima has as its obverse the notion that it is very good indeed to try to know all that we should know. There is, in fact, a salutary humility to be gained in the experience of being brought up against the limits of our knowledge, the point beyond which we cannot seek to know, where we must patiently wait to be told. "To se muche and suffre moore, certes is dowel!" (B.XI.412).

Intellectualism, pro- and anti-, is thus basically ambivalent. As was the case with Lady Meed, the ambivalence of value is rendered by an ambivalence of the character embodying that value. Dame Study, the domineering wife of Wit, describes and exemplifies in her person the virtue of *studiositas* and the opposed though complementary vice of *curiositas*.[1] On the one hand, she is stern in her condemnation of an irreverent approach to intellectual matters; on the other, she is susceptible to flattery, relenting immediately to the dreamer's "mekenesse . . . and . . . mylde speche" (B.X.152). She condemns those whose curiosity about God's ways with men leads them and those who hear them into skepticism:

> Swiche motyues þei meue, þise maistres in hir glorie,
> And maken men in mys bileue þat muse on hire wordes.
> Ymaginatif herafterward shal answere to youre purpos.
> Austyn to swiche Argueres he telleþ þis teme:
> *Non plus sapere quam oportet.*
>
> . . . .
>
> For alle þat wilneþ to wite þe whyes of god almyȝty,
> I wolde his eiȝe were in his ers and his hele after."
> (B.X.117–21, 127–28)[2]

Although she clearly states the proper intellectual humility of *studiositas*, Dame Study does not simply personify this virtue. Instead, she personifies the intellectual activity that this virtue should govern. As such she is ambivalent and, by the end of her second speech, she can slide into the opposed vice of *curiositas*. After condemning alchemy

1. Common terms in medieval discussions of virtues. See, for example, Saint Thomas, *Summa Theologiae*, 2–2.166, 167.
2. The lines about "Ymaginatif" are not in A. Langland had not thought his way through to the solutions offered by this personification in B.XII.

and astronomy and the like as obstacles to "Dowel," she confesses (or boasts): "Alle þise Sciences I myself sotilede and ordeynede, / Founded hem formest folk to deceyue" (B.X.220–21).

An interesting parallel to Study's double nature is to be found in Hunger, the personification called in by Piers to discipline the loafers on his half-acre (B.VI.171ff.). Hunger knocks some of the fat off them, and has everyone working hard to avoid his attacks. In the course of his stay he gives Piers some very good advice on work and moderation. When Piers suggests that Hunger might leave now that he has accomplished his purpose, Hunger asks for a meal. Piers gives him what humble fare his workers can bring:

> Hunger eet þis in haste and axed after moore.
> .   .   .   .
> Thanne was folk fayn and fedde hunger wiþ þe beste;
> Wiþ good Ale as Gloton taȝte þei garte hym to slepe.
>
> (B.VI.296, 300–301)

Like Study, Hunger practically turns into his own opposite before he leaves the poem. Hunger and Study are both disciplines. Hunger forces the irresponsible loafers to get to work as they should. Study tames the irresponsible play of the intellect by subjecting it to the demands of different kinds of learning and crafts; this is the point of her rebuke to Wit. But the full success of the industry that Hunger inspires brings with it a reversion to the sorry condition he was called upon to cure; and the full mastery of the disciplines of Study makes the intellect capable of subtler and more dangerous irresponsibilities. To adopt Donaldson's remarks on another character, each of these personifications is "an entity with extension in two directions, while a human being is an entity with extension in an infinite number of directions. One does not ordinarily label each of the various extensions of a man, but one may of a personification."[3] The dialectic I have stated discursively here is just such a labeling of what Study and Hunger embody poetically.

The dangers of intellectualism were, of course, always of concern to theologians. Saint Augustine and others gave grudging approval to secular learning, but only as an aid to the study of the Bible. The

---

3. Donaldson, *C-Text*, p. 174, referring to Recklessness in his expanded role in C.

patristic rationalization of learning was, as E. R. Curtius tells us, "that Greek learning was established by God: the Christian teacher needed it in order to understand the Scriptures." There were allegorical readings of Scripture to support this. For instance, Saint Augustine said that just as the Israelites took gold and silver vessels with them when they went out of Egypt (Exod. 3:22 and 12:35), so Christians must rid pagan learning of what is pernicious so that they can put it to the service of truth.[4] Cassiodorus, in his *Institutiones divinarum et secularium litteratum*, went so far as to argue that the seeds of the pagan liberal arts are to be found in God's wisdom and in Scripture, and that, in dim antiquity, the Greeks actually found them there. He quotes Psalm 19:1–4 (Authorized Version): "The heavens declare the glory of God. . . . There is no speech nor language where their voice is not heard . . . their words are gone out through all the world. . . ." This means, allegorically, that "the Old Testament was known to all peoples." Thus, from the Old Testament, "the pagans could learn all the arts of rhetoric and reduce them to a system"![5]

The seven liberal arts, composed of the trivium—grammar, dialectic or logic, and rhetoric—and the quadrivium—music, arithmetic, geometry, and astronomy—formed the basis of medieval education; and, by such arguments as those of Cassiodorus, they were not only rendered innocuous but were positively sanctified by their association with Scripture. This association was only beginning to be called into question in Langland's time, when secular learning seemed ready to trade its adopted sanctity for greater autonomy. The older tradition is clearly reflected in Study's directions to the dreamer:

> "I shal kenne þee to my Cosyn þat Clergie is hoten.
> He haþ wedded a wif wiþInne þise woukes six,
> Is sib to þe seuen artȝ, þat Scripture is nempned.
> They two, as I hope, after my bisechyng,
> Shullen wissen þee to dowel, I dar wel vndertake."
>
> (B.X.153–57)

"Clergye," of course, means "Learning," and it is important not to confuse it with the modern meaning of "clergy." However, we should also realize the inadequacy of "Learning" to render the full sense of the Middle English word; for there is in "Clergye" a connotation of

---

4. Curtius, *European Literature*, pp. 39, 40.
5. Ibid., p. 41. For the passages in Cassiodorus see *PL* 70:19–21.

holiness, almost a sacramental character, that any modern rendering
of its denotation must lack.[6] We are no longer accustomed to think
of Learning as married to the inspired word of God. The total integra-
tion of man's religious, intellectual, and craftsmanlike efforts which
this marriage implies is impressively demonstrated in Study's list of
services rendered:

"So shaltow come to Clergie þat kan manye wittes.
Seye hym þis signe: I sette hym to Scole,
And þat I grete wel his wif, for I wroot hire þe bible,
And sette hire to Sapience and to þe Sauter glosed.
Logyk I lerned hire, and al þe lawe after,
And alle þe Musons in Musik I made hire to knowe.
Plato þe poete, I putte hym first to boke;
Aristotle and oþere mo to argue I tauȝte;
Grammer for girles I garte first write,
And bette hem wiþ a baleys but if þei wolde lerne.
Of alle kynne craftes I contreued tooles,
Of Carpenters and kerueres; I kenned first Masons
And lerned hem leuel and lyne þouȝ I loke dymme."
                                         (B.X.172–84)

A precedent for this more extensive list of arts can be found in *The
Didascalicon* of Hugh of Saint Victor, where we find the seven "mechanical arts"—fabric making, armament, commerce, and the like—
integrated into a system which includes theology, physics, and the
seven liberal arts. The system is traced back as a whole directly to
the divine Wisdom, and its study is intended "to restore within us the
divine likeness, a likeness which to us is a form but to God is his
nature."[7]

Study's discussion of Theology shows her awareness of this final
goal which lies just beyond her grasp:

6. Erzgräber, *William Langlands Piers Plowman*, p. 122, says that Clergy
represents spiritual learning, going back to the Church Fathers, while Study
represents natural learning; but this squares neither with Study's claim that
she taught Scripture nor with Clergy's acknowledgment of the seven liberal
arts as his "sons," and of the limits of his knowledge (B.XIII.119–30; C.XVI.
129–37).

7. *Didascalicon* 2.1, trans. Taylor, p. 61. For a list of all the branches of
study, see 3.1, p. 82.

"Ac Theologie haþ tened me ten score tymes;
The moore I muse þerInne þe mystier it semeþ,
And þe depper I deuyned þe derker me þouȝte.
It is no Science forsoþe for to sotile Inne;
Ne were þe loue þat liþ þerinne a well lewed þyng it were.
Ac for it leteþ best bi loue I loue it þe bettre,
For þere þat loue is ledere lakkeþ neuere grace.
Loke þow loue lelly if þee likeþ dowel,
For dobet and dobest ben drawen of loues scole.

.　.　.　.　.　.　.　.　.

Forþi loke þow louye as longe as þow durest,
For is no science vnder sonne so souereyn for þe soule."

(B.X.185–93, 210–11)

The arts and learning finally resolve themselves into love, which goes
beyond their reach into mystery. We have here a variation on the
theme of Lady Holy Church's speech. If we recall how love in that
speech is identified with Love, the Incarnate Christ, we can see in this
speech of Study's the logic of the transition from the *Vita de Dowel*
to the *Vita de Dobet*. For in this transition the dreamer advances
through the arts and learning to the point where they must yield in
confusion to the paradox of the Incarnation, a mystery of Love.

This sort of progress of the arts to their own confusion is a favorite
theme of medieval literature. Virgil's guidance of Dante to the
threshold of Paradise but not beyond is only the most celebrated example. In Alain de Lille's *Anticlaudian* (ca. 1182–83), the Goddess
Natura sends Prudence, Phronesis (i.e., Wisdom), and Reason as
envoys to ask God's help in the creation of a perfect man. They are
equipped with a carriage built by the seven arts and drawn by the five
senses, but as they approach the throne of God Prudence and Phronesis must leave the carriage and Reason behind, submitting to the
guidance of Theology and Faith. A description of the Blessed Virgin
in heaven, which was often excerpted and may have been used by
Dante, uses paradox to show the defeat of the arts in the mystery of
the Virgin Birth: "No longer do 'mother' and 'virgin' disagree, but
turn to kisses of peace, that strife of theirs shut out. Here Nature is
silent, Logic's force is banished, all of Rhetoric's authority falls, and
Reason totters."[8] It is important to remember that this defeat of

8. *Anticlaudian* 5.9, in *PL* 210:538 B, C.

learning does not deny learning its proper value. In Alain de Lille as in Langland, it is learning that brings man to the brink of transcendent vision. Paradox, after all, is eminently intellectual. It is a symbol of the restless workings of the human mind engaged in study and constantly subverting its own supposedly firm conclusions with new alternatives. It is thought caught in motion. The Incarnation is a paradox brought forth into the objective order. It is the visible encounter of God and man and an endorsement of the very intellectualism it transcends, an idea best illustrated in the last canto of Dante's *Paradiso* where the poet's efforts to comprehend the Incarnation are compared to a geometer's efforts to square the circle.

The general tradition of divine illumination in which Langland seems to participate grounds the works of the intellect in the Word of God "who illumines every man who comes into the world" (John 1.9). Study confirms this when she says that love is the best of sciences, and the proper ground of all the other sciences. So does Patience when, later in the poem, he says that Dowel is teaching and loving, and gives as his directions thereto a riddle that engages the intellect only to confuse it. Since to do well is to pursue the sciences and arts to their foundation, the dreamer must move beyond Study to Clergy and Scripture.

His argument with these two figures brings on the crisis that interrupted the A-text and remains something of a muddle in B and C. When the dreamer asks Clergy for his definitions of Do-well, Do-bet, and Do-best, Clergy replies that Do-well is common belief in the teachings of the Church; Do-bet is practicing what you preach; and Do-best is boldly to blame the guilty, but only when you yourself are guiltless (B.X.238–39, 257–60, 264–76). The importance and difficulty of this last condition are stressed so much that it seems it will be fulfilled only when the apocalyptic king arrives to reform monasteries and give a knock to the abbot of Abingdon. That passage, which we have discussed and which C incorporates into Reason's speech in the *Visio*, is intimately connected with Clergy's idea of the value of learning in society. We see this in his description of what a house of learning should be, and of what it is in these bad times which call out for the reforms of the avenging king:

"For if heuene be on þis erþe, and ese to any soule,
It is in cloistre or in scole, by manye skiles I fynde.
For in cloistre comeþ no man to carpe ne to fiʒte

But al is buxomnesse þere and bokes, to rede and to lerne.
In scole þere is scorn but if a clerk wol lerne,
And great loue and likyng for ech loweþ hym to oother.
Ac now is Religion a rydere, a rennere by stretes,
A ledere of loudayes and a lond buggere,
A prikere on a palfrey fro place to Manere,
An heep of houndes at his ers as he a lord were."

(B.X.305–14)

R. E. Kaske has found a probable source for the lines about the school as a heaven on earth in a saying attributed to Peter Damian: "Si paradisus in hoc mundo est, in claustro vel in scholis est."[9] Morton Bloomfield claims a more general relevance for this monastic notion of the *"Paradisus claustralis,"* the earthly paradise which is "the image of the heavenly paradise, and [whose] inhabitants are similarly angels or beatified souls. Earthly paradise is also an image of the pure soul, the paradise within perhaps not happier but at least as happy as the eternal one."[10] Here, as in the political ideas we discussed in the last chapter, the activities of the human mind find their expression and image in an institution, a corporate entity. Intellectual incoherence is thus a corollary of institutional incoherence now that "Religion [is] a rydere, a rennere by stretes."

Learning is always a corporate enterprise, undertaken by the "community of scholars." The cooperation of minds in pursuit of truth is a natural model for the ideal state where political man cooperates with his fellows in pursuing other aspects of truth. So Clergy's aspirations have a social dimension, seeking their fruition in the advent of that apocalyptic king. It is understandable that the dreamer's tentative summary of Clergy's lesson should lean too far in the political direction: " 'Thanne is dowel and dobet,' quod I, *'dominus* and knyʒthode?' " (B.X.336). Scripture's rebuke of the dreamer, however, seems to go beyond his distortion and to threaten the very substance of Clergy's teaching. We here begin that series of contradictions that makes Passūs X and XI so hard to follow.

Scripture denies that political structures have any relevance to salvation:

9. "Langland and the *Paradisus Claustralis," Modern Language Notes* 72 (1957):482. The saying is attributed to "Petrus Ravennus" (probably Peter Damian) by Benvenuto da Imola in his commentary on Dante.

10. *Apocalypse*, p. 47.

"I nel noȝt scorne," quod Scripture; "but scryueynes lye,
Kynghod and knyȝthod, for auȝt I kan awayιe,
Helpeþ noȝt to heueneward at oone yeris ende,
Ne richesse ne rentes ne Reautee of lordes.
Poule preueþ it impossible, riche men in heuene;
Salomon seiþ also þat siluer is worst to louye."

(B.X.337–42)

Scripture introduces here the theme of patient poverty which will dominate subsequent passages of the *Vita de Dowel*. Now patient poverty as an ideal is certainly not incompatible with the program of Clergy, but the dismissal of "Kynghod" and "knyȝthod" does seem to be. Scripture's concept of salvation is more radical and individual than Clergy's. It makes no allowance for the beneficent influence of institutions. Yet the two ideals depend on each other. If learning is to be authentic, it must remain in touch with its biblical inspiration. If the word of God is to maintain its presence in the world, it must work through the institutions of the Earthly City which foster and protect learning, even though its message is, in great part, a rejection of these institutions as repositories of real value. Will's inability to deal with this apparent contradiction shows plainly in his responses to both his instructors.

When Clergy gives his definitions of the three Do's, Will's response is reductive. He identifies Do-well and Do-bet with *dominus* and knighthood, seizing on the political superstructure instead of the heart of Clergy's ideal vision, the school whose pursuit of truth in love is a heaven on earth. For Clergy, as for Conscience in his grammatical analogy, *dominus* and knighthood are not valuable in themselves but only in so far as they are the symbol of "god, the grounde of al, a graciouse antecedent" (C.IV.356). As Thought has also explained, the king is chosen to protect the Church, which includes the institutions of Clergy and which is the more perfect reflection of the divine order. When Scripture gives her guide to salvation, with its disdain for institutions and its emphasis on the individual, Will's response is likewise reductive. Scripture has denied that the rich have "Eritage in heuene" as do the patient poor. They enter it not by right but only by "ruþe and grace."

"*Contra!*" quod I, "by crist! þat kan I wiþseye,
And preuen it by þe pistel þat Peter is nempned:
That is baptiȝed beþ saaf, be he riche or pouere."

(B.X.349–51)

Just as he pushed Clergy's institutionalism beyond Clergy's substantive intentions, so now the dreamer pushes Scripture's individualism beyond her intentions. Where we might expect his "*contra*" to be a defense of the goodness of wealth rightly used, the dreamer argues instead for the total irrelevance of *any* good works to salvation. If the relationship of the individual man to God is a mystery of grace which is not signified by public institutions, then perhaps it is not signified even by the good works and virtues which have consequence and meaning in this world.

Most of the dreamer's subsequent speech is an attack on the value of learning, but this seems to be part of a more general attack on the value of good works. Langland considered learning to be one species of good works, and he has his dreamer interpret Ecclesiastes 9:1— "*Sunt iusti atque sapientes; et opera eorum in manu dei sunt*"—to show the tenuous relationship of both to salvation (B.X.436–47). And so the damnation of Aristotle and the salvation of the good thief are adduced to show the doubtful relevance of good works in a scheme of salvation that seems to have been determined "In þe legende of lif longe er I were" (B.X.381). All human endeavor is invalidated by the economy of grace, and the least learned of men gain salvation with a prayer:

Ne none sonner saued, ne sadder of bileue,
Than Plowmen and pastours and pouere commune laborers,
Souteres and shepherdes; swiche lewed Iuttes
Percen wiþ a Paternoster þe paleys of heuene
And passen Purgatorie penauncelees at hir hennes partyng
Into þe parfit blisse of Paradis for hir pure bileue,
That inparfitly here knewe and ek lyuede.

(B.X.465–71)

These appealing lines are true in part, and herein lies the complication, because they form the conclusion of an argument the poem will substantially reject.

———

Scripture rejects the argument immediately and her rejection drives the dreamer "for wo and wraþe of hir speche" (B.XI.4) into a dream within a dream. This may, paradoxically, cloak events in Langland's real life when he turned from dreaming and from writing after frustration with the A-text. The obscurity of Passus XI is doubly tantalizing because one feels that here more than elsewhere in the poem Langland registers the confusion engendered by the theological controversies of his day. It is difficult to say just what he registers and how, for at least two reasons other than his evasive presentation. First, "the intellectual life of the period," according to one of its leading historians, "is everywhere still largely veiled in mists; but in England the obscurity is nearer to fog."[11] The second reason, an intrinsic one, is that Langland does not have Dante's taste for systematic exposition. He prefers instead to record his vivid impressions of the intellectual life around him in a poetically consistent order not traceable to Augustine or Bonaventure or Bradwardine or Ockham.

Let us consider, first, two passages already summarized from Passus X, in which Will calls into question the value of knowledge and good works. In the first, Will says that Scripture contains "tales" of man's predestination, suggesting

> þat I man maad was, and my name yentred
> In þe legende of lif longe er I were,
> Or ellis vnwriten for wikkednesse as holy writ witnesseþ:
> *Nemo ascendit ad celum nisi qui de celo descendit.*
>   (B.X.380–83)[12]

According to this view, man's good works and bad works are determined by God's foreknowledge of them. This foreknowledge is attested by the prophets in Scripture, and the problem of predestination was closely connected in the fourteenth century with "any serious discussion of the authority and infallibility of Scripture."[13] The doctrine

11. Gordon Leff, *Bradwardine and the Pelagians* (Cambridge: Cambridge University Press, 1957), p. 1. The suggestion that the inner dream was a veiled autobiography of the years between the A- and B-texts was made by R. W. Chambers, *Man's Unconquerable Mind*, pp. 135–36. Wittig suggests that "the forty-five years Will sees himself disport in the 'londe of Longynge' need not be thought of as actually elapsing *while* Will is dreaming. . . . The foreshortened time suggests rather that Langland is emphasizing a kind of retrospective re-evaluation. . . . Langland wishes to summarize dramatically all that is wrong with Will's life" ("Inward Journey," p. 245). Wittig generally regards the questions of predestination, grace, and merit as trivial evasions on Will's part of his clear moral duty. As my subsequent discussion will show, I believe Langland took these matters more seriously, and this is probably my most important difference with Wittig on this part of the poem.

12. The Latin text is John 3:13.

13. W. A. Pantin, *The English Church in the Fourteenth Century* (Cambridge: Cambridge University Press, 1955), p. 131. This problem of "future

is grim enough, certainly, but it does preserve the significance of good
and bad works in the scheme of salvation, even if it removes them
from the scope of free will. Determinism is, if nothing else, thor-
oughly intelligible. The second passage carries the train of thought
further, to an unexpected conclusion:

> That Salomon seiþ I trowe be sooþ and certein of vs alle:
> *Sunt iusti atque sapientes, & opera eorum in manu dei sunt &c.*
> Ther are witty and wel libbynge ac hire werkes ben yhudde
> In þe hondes of almyȝty god, and he woot þe soþe
> Wher for loue a man worþ allowed þere and hise lele werkes,
> Or ellis for his yuel wille and enuye of herte,
> And be allowed as he lyued so; for by luþere men knoweþ þe
> goode.
> And wherby wiste men which is whit if alle þynge blak were,
> And who were a good man but if þer were som sherewe?
> Forþi lyue we forþ wiþ liþere men; I leue fewe ben goode,
> For *quant oportet vient en place yl nyad que pati.*
> And he þat may al amende haue mercy on vs alle,
> For soþest word þat euer god seide was þo he seide *Nemo bonus.*
>   (B.X.436–47)

The most striking development here is that Will is no longer talking
about who will be saved and who will be damned. He restricts himself to the saved and contrasts the reasons for their salvation. Some
might be saved because of their good works. Others might be saved
because of, or despite, their wickedness. Middle English "for" (1.
440) is ambiguous, and Langland may be exploiting its ambiguity.
"Despite" is the gloss required by our sense of the limits of Christian
heterodoxy, but "because of" seems favored by the parallel structure
(". . . for loue . . . for his yuel wille . . ."). Either way the doctrine
is unsettling. We should not allow ourselves to be misled by the fact
that Will's examples—Mary Magdalen, David, the good thief, and
others—repented before they died. In the dramatic context of the
poem Will misuses these examples by de-emphasizing this detail.
Langland the poet allows him to do so and allows us to see it. What

contingents" is also discussed by Leff in *Bradwardine,* passim, and in *Richard
Fitzralph, Commentator of the Sentences* (Manchester: Manchester University
Press, 1963), pp. 39ff.; and by Copleston, *A History of Philosophy,* 3:37–39,
92–93.

Will comes up with is a complete moral indeterminism as regards salvation. God might, in His absolute freedom, save men "for" their very wickedness because it serves as a foil for others' goodness. Salvation is simply a function of His pleasure in a kind of moral chiaroscuro. No wonder Will throws up his hands and dismisses learning which Christ commended but little, settling instead for the simple faith which pierces "wiþ a Paternoster þe paleys of heuene."

What results, however, is not a life of simple virtue, but a carrying into practice of Will's theoretical indeterminism. The inner dream, which seems to cloak the poet's wayward waking life, is governed by Fortune, the personification of all that is random and unintelligible to the Middle Ages:

> A merueillous metels mette me þanne,
> For I was rauysshed riȝt þere; Fortune me fette
> And into þe lond of longynge and loue she me brouȝte
> And in a Mirour þat hiȝte middelerþe she made me biholde.
> Siþen she seide to me, "here myȝtow se wondres
> And knowe þat þow coueitest and come þerto paraunter."

(B.XI.6–11)

The "lond of longynge and loue" suggests Saint Bernard's *regio dissimilitudinis* where man wanders in his estrangement from God. The "Mirour þat hiȝte middelerþe" parodies a favorite title for both mystical and encyclopedic works of the Middle Ages. Instead of a *Speculum Historiale* or a *Speculum Charitatis* it is a *Speculum Hujus Mundi*. Instead of mirroring God in his creation as these other *Specula* do, it simply mirrors man in his cupidity, to the exclusion of anything higher.[14] The point is that if God is so unintelligible in His dealings with man, if His creation is so devoid of any order, including the ethical, then His creation simply cannot mirror Him.

Let us turn now to the learned controversies of Langland's day and see if we can trace his dilemma to some of its sources. The cen-

---

14. On the *regio dissimilitudinis*, see Gilson, *The Mystical Theology of Saint Bernard*, pp. 45–46; Pierre Courcelle, *Les Confessions de Saint Augustin dans la tradition littéraire: Antécédents et Postérité* (Paris: Études Augustiniennes, 1963), pp. 278–88, 623–40; applications to *Piers Plowman* are found in Vasta, *Spiritual Basis*, pp. 76–77, and Wittig, pp. 232–35. Helmut Maisack, *William Langlands Verhältnis zum Zisterziensischen Mönchtum* (Balingen: n.p., 1953), p. 40, links the "myroure that hiȝt Mydlerd" to the *speculum* tradition. See, also, Wittig, pp. 238–41.

tral fact of intellectual life in the fourteenth century was the break between theology and philosophy, a break which, in Langland's terms, could be called the divorce of Clergy and Scripture. The last great synthesis, that of Thomas Aquinas, had allowed to each field a novel degree of autonomy, but had insisted on their ultimate harmony. For Thomas, the truths of reason were intelligible without reference to the truths of revelation. The truths of revelation, if they exceeded those of reason, still did not contradict them. Among the truths of reason were those which pertained to ethics and the right ordering of our lives. Now our good works could not of themselves merit the reward of union with God. This depended on our possession of grace, a freely bestowed gift. But once we possessed grace, we could discover by our reason what acts would help us to grow in it and what would cause us to lose it. Ethics, rationally evolved, was the way to the perfection of that human nature which exists as an idea in the creative mind of God.[15] It was the human share in the scheme of salvation, a scheme to which God Himself was metaphysically bound.

And there was the rub. Can God be bound? The response of piety, jealous of God's omnipotence, was no. If the intelligibility of creation and of God's will for us was to be won only at the cost of His freedom, then it had to be foregone. The first notable challenges to the continuity of human and divine minds came in 1277 with the condemnations at Paris and Oxford of several Thomistic positions, on the grounds that they subjected God to an Aristotelian determinism. At the turn of the fourteenth century the Franciscan Duns Scotus attacked the Thomistic notion of the analogy of being. Thomas had secured our relation to God by comparing the reality, or being, of our separate essences to the being of God which *was* His essence, and was the source of all being in others. Scotus also rejected Thomas's method of starting with sensible creation and moving by a chain of causes back to God. True to the Augustinian and Bonaventurian tendencies of his order, he made God's will the "measure of all that He did,"[16] and made all that links man to God a matter of freely elected love on both sides. This emphasis on will over intellect is certainly reflected in Langland, as Willi Erzgräber has argued,[17] but Scotus cannot qualify as a definitive influence because he severed one more link which

15. Thomas's teaching on divine ideas was derived from Saint Augustine, not from Aristotle, as Copleston notes in *A History of Philosophy*, 2:427.
16. Leff, *Bradwardine*, p. 7.
17. *William Langlands Piers Plowman*, pp. 190ff.

Langland considered precious: the divine illumination of the intellect. This was a break with Augustinianism, despite Scotus's claims to the contrary.[18]

The discontinuity thus introduced between God and man was nearly complete, and the work was finished by the thinker "who for keenness of mind and ruthlessness surpassed all his contemporaries,"[19] William of Ockham. Ockham's famous razor cut through all sorts of continuities in the medieval world, on the general principle that there are no real relations between things, only rational or logical ones.[20] In this new universe of discrete particulars the universal concept lost even the carefully restricted validity granted it by Thomism. An idea like "man" or "human nature" no longer represented a real nature common to two particular men; it represented no single idea in the mind of God according to which He created them. It was simply a term used to express our perception of similarities between men. No binding, certain moral law, valid for all men, could be erected on such a shaky foundation. In the terms of Will's complaint to Lady Holy Church, man could have no "kynde knowyng" of "Dowel." The moral law came to depend, for Ockham more than for Scotus, on the absolutely free will of God operating without even the restraint of divine ideas. In other words, God does not forbid one act and reward another because they are wrong or right in themselves; rather, an act is wrong or right because God forbids or rewards it.[21]

The denial of real relations between entities applied as well to the relation of rational creatures to God. Ockham and his followers denied the ontological status of grace as an essential constituent of merit, saying that it was simply a name for the fact of God's acceptance of man.[22] This, combined with the Ockhamists' insistence on the

18. See Gilson, *Jean Duns Scot* (Paris: J. Vrin, 1952), pp. 556–73, esp. 559–60.

19. David Knowles, "A Characteristic of the Mental Climate of the Four-teenth Century," in *Mélanges Offerts à Étienne Gilson* (Paris and Toronto: Pontifical Institute of Mediaeval Studies and J. Vrin, 1959), p. 321.

20. Ockham's razor was the axiom *entia non sunt multiplicanda extra neces-sitatem*, which he did not himself formulate, but which does accurately de-scribe his practice. Ibid., p. 322.

21. Copleston suggests that this implies "the possibility of two ethics, the moral order established by God but knowable only by revelation, and a pro-visional and second-class natural and non-theological ethic worked out by the human reason without revelation" (*A History of Philosophy*, 3:14).

22. "Item ex actibus meritoriis generatur habitus inclinans ad consimiles actus, igitur sicut potest acceptare secundum actum elicitum mediante habitu: ita primum et per consequens potest acceptare actum sine habitu naturalem

absolute power of God, had a dual consequence. On earth, man's free will was given a fuller scope in that it could merit God's favor on its own. But in heaven, on the other hand, God's absolute freedom meant that He could choose at random those acts and those men who would be pleasing to Him. The resulting indeterminism was at once exhilarating and terrifying.

The emphasis in Ockham's own teaching, as Gordon Leff has shown, was on the exhilarating extension of the free will's scope of action, and here, as we shall see, Langland and he find common grounds of hope. Ockham said that "merit is the cause *sine qua non* of reward and grace" from God.[23] This practically reversed the traditional priority whereby grace, a supernatural habit or quality of the soul, was the condition *sine qua non* of merit. It meant that the act of man's free will was the first step, the origin of merit, to which God freely responded. But even in Ockham the corollary was to be found that God could "condemn" a man "without any fault of his own."[24] Or, more chillingly: "Grace and glory are two effects produced by God; grace is prior because it is in the soul in its earthly life [*in viatore*], and glory is posterior because it is in the final union with God [*in consummatione*]. So God could confer grace and charity on someone and not confer glory . . . indeed, God can, in His absolute power, confer charity on someone and then annihilate him."[25] Now Ockham did not think that God would act with such arbitrary tyranny,

sine actu infuso." *Quaestiones et decisiones in IV libros Sententiarum Petri Lombardi* 3, qu. 5 I (Lyons, 1495), cited and discussed in Leff, *Bradwardine*, p. 196, n.2. I have compared Leff's quotations with a copy of Ockham's commentary in the Beinecke Rare Book Library, Yale University. I have made (and noted) a few minor corrections in the following citations.

23. "Sed meritum non est nisi causa sine qua non respectu premii et gratie." *Quaestiones et decisiones* 4, qu. 1 E, quoted in Leff, *Bradwardine*, p. 204, n.1.

24. Cited in A. Pelzer, "Les 51 Articles de Guillaume Occam censurés en Avignon en 1326," *Revue d'histoire ecclésiastique* 18 (1922):253; and in Leff, *Bradwardine*, p. 192, n.1.

25. ". . . gratia et gloria sunt duo effectus producti a deo; gratia est prior, quare est in viatore, et gloria est posterior, quia est in consummatione, igitur potest deus conferre alicui gratiam et caritatem et non conferre sibi gloriam . . . non obstante quod conferat sibi gratiam . . . viatori cuicumque potest deus conferre gratiam et caritatem et statim post potest eum annihilare, et per consequens potest sibi conferre gratiam et dispositionem et eum annihilare. . . .

"Ideo dico . . . ad istam conclusionem quod caritas nec quecunque alius habitus necessitet deum ad dandum alicui vitam eternam; imo de potentia absoluta potest alicui conferre caritatem et eum post annihilare" (*Quaestiones et decisiones* 3, qu. 5 E and H). Quoted in Leff, *Bradwardine*, p. 195, n.2. Leff omits "deus" in its second occurrence and has "potest" for "post" in the last line.

but his cutting away of the certitudes that the Middle Ages had placed between God and man gave a new emphasis to the fact that He could.

This emphasis was more nearly central to the thought of Ockham's followers Robert Holkot and Adam of Woodham. Holkot said that all merit came from the creature's conformity to divine law, but that a creature could not be sure "that some particular law is ordained by God, for God could allow man to be without any law . . . just as He does with beasts, if it pleased His will."[26] Once again, there can be no "kynde knowing" of "Dowel." God, said Holkot, could give grace to a man and damn him. He could save a man in mortal sin, and thus prove that "a man who loves God the less is loved by God the more." Finally, "God can accept for eternal life all the natural acts of man, and He can also make all free acts indifferent or non-meritorious."[27] Adam of Woodham went so far as to say that God could allow grace and mortal sin to exist in the same person.[28] He found it even more

26. In citing Holkot I have consulted a reprint of the edition cited by Leff, Robertus Holkot, *In Quatuor Libros Sententiarum Quaestiones*, Lugduni, 1518, Unveränderte Nachdruck (Frankfurt, 1967), as well as another edition, *Magistri Roberti holkot Super quattuor libros sententiarum questiones . . .* (Lyons, 1505), in the Beinecke Library. The first text cited follows, with Leff's readings in brackets: ". . . omne meritum vel demeritum est ex hoc quod actus creature est conformis vel difformis legi divine: ideo enim homo meretur: quia facit sicut deus vult eum facere . . . et ideo demeretur quia facit contrarium legi divine, sed non est in potestate voluntatis create [creature] quod sibi aliqua lex a deo ponatur, posset enim deus permittere hominem sine lege sibi data et sine preceptis vel consiliis: sicut permittit [permittet] bestias: si voluntati sue placeret" (1, qu. 1, art. 2 D). Quoted in Leff, *Bradwardine*, p. 219, n.1.

27. ". . . dico quod ista consequentia non valet: deus infundit charitatem isti: vel auget seu [vel] conservat in isto scilicet *a* charitatem: et in *b* non [et non *b*]: ergo magis diligit [diliget] *a* quam *b*: quia capio unum prescitum [praescitum] ad mortem eternam existentem in gratia: et alium predestinatum [praedestinatum] existentem in peccato mortali: istum plus diligit: manifestum est. . . . Secundo dico quod consequens non est inconveniens, videlicet quod minus diligens deum plus diligatur a deo . . ." (1, qu. 4, art. 3 H). ". . . deus potest acceptare ad vitam eternam omnes actus naturales alicuius hominis: et facere omnes actus liberos atque indifferentes aut non meritorios . . ." (1, qu. 1, art. 4 [4D in Leff; I find no marginal D opposite this passage, lines 11–14 of art. 4]). Quoted in Leff, *Bradwardine*, p. 217, nn.2, 3. In the first passage "predestinatum" means predestined for glory and "prescitum" means predestined for damnation; both are common usages.

28. "Ad istud respondeo quod non dixi quod aliquis habens gratiam increatam secundum quam deus secundum presentem iustitiam acceptat ad vitam eternam, possit cum hoc esse in culpa mortali de dei potentia absoluta sed dictum est quod gratia informans non habet formalem repugnantiam ex natura sua ad culpam mortalem . . . et ideo dicendum quod non starent simul hec duo: iste habet gratiam et iste peccat mortaliter, nec huic repugnat hec quod dixi, scilicet quod gratia creata non repugnat ex natura sua culpe mortali vel

difficult—Gordon Leff suggests he found it impossible—to establish any link whatever between the human act and the divine response. The human will can merit without grace, but "there can be an act not meritorious and yet good in kind and nature."[29] All this approaches rather closely the skepticism of Will's rebuke to Scripture and seems to sanction the wayward life of the inner dream.

This was a century of intellectual extremes, and so the reaction to Ockhamist indeterminism was the bleak, total determinism of Thomas Bradwardine. In *De Causa Dei* (ca. 1344) he "erected his system of determinist theology which departs from orthodoxy in one direction almost as clearly as do the 'Pelagians', whom he was attacking, in another."[30] He reinstated grace as a necessary cause of salvation, a return to Augustinian orthodoxy from the position of the Ockhamists. He went a good deal further, though, by making God a "senior partner in all that concerns His creatures,"[31] including the individual acts of the human will by which man grows in grace or loses it. God became the human will's "first and most immediate mover,"[32] eliminating merit as previously understood. The freedom of the human will consisted for Bradwardine in nothing more than its direct subjugation to God's will, itself absolutely free.[33] Though Bradwardine sought to exclude the possibility, a French theologian was able to cite him, some ten or twelve years after his death, as an authority for the doctrine that God's will can cause man to sin.[34] Indeed, given Bradwardine's premises, the position is plausible. Another, more important vessel of his influence in Langland's England was John Wyclif, whose predestinarianism was, unlike Bradwardine's, partly metaphysical in origin, but who paid him the tribute of the title "Doctor Profundus"

---

quod potest simul stare de dei potentia absoluta cum culpa mortali . . ." (*Super sententias* 1, dis. 17, qu. 3). Cited from MSS in Leff, *Bradwardine*, p. 245, n.4. Note that "gratia increata" means the actual acceptance for salvation of a soul by God; "gratia creata" means the supernatural habit of grace in the soul of one not yet saved, synonymous with "gratia informans."

29. "Licet non meritorium sed bonum ex genere et natura actus [*sic*]" (*Super sententias* 1, dist. 17, qu. 1). Quoted in Leff, *Bradwardine*, p. 247, n.6.

30. M. D. Knowles, "The Censured Opinions of Uthred of Boldon," *Proceedings of the British Academy* 38 (1951): 308.

31. Leff, *Bradwardine*, p. 15.

32. Ibid., p. 95.

33. Ibid., pp. 91ff.

34. Pierre de Ceffons argued thus "in his highly Ockhamist sentences (Paris, c. 1360)." J. A. Robson, *Wyclif and the Oxford Schools* (Cambridge: Cambridge University Press, 1961), p. 40. Cf. Leff, *Bradwardine*, pp. 95–96.

and attacked his Ockhamist opponents under the same name, "Pelagians."[35]

My sketch of these two opposed views of the human will, grace, and salvation has been only a rough one. Indeed, it may be so rough as to suggest that they had more in common than at issue. This seems to have been Langland's view, as we see when he slides so easily from one position to another in the long tirade of Passus X. Both schools had rendered highly problematic the notion of the human will's cooperation with grace. Both took man's most vital concern, his salvation, out of his control, and this included the control exercised by learning and knowing the created order.

Historically, two complementary effects flowed from this loss of control. The first was a remarkable development of logic and mathematics, those studies which make the least claims to any truth beyond their arbitrary premises.[36] The second effect was the development of mysticism. As is well known, the fourteenth century witnessed a florescence of mystical writing in England, and one of its common notes is a distrust of learning or knowledge. Julian of Norwich refers to herself as "unlettered," and whatever the historical value of this characterization, its significance as a rhetorical pose is unambiguous. It is to such humble and unlettered ones that God grants the extraordinary grace of His "showings," and the nonrational assurances that "all shall be well, and all shall be well, and all manner of thing shall be well" as regards man's salvation.[37] The author of *The Cloud of Unknowing* calls on those who would advance to God to lay a "cloud of forgetting" over all God's creation:

35. Robson discusses Wyclif's relation to Bradwardine on pp. 179–214; see esp. 210–14.

36. Philotheus Boehner, O.F.M., *Medieval Logic* (Chicago: University of Chicago Press, 1952), p. 95, argues that the logic of this period has a great deal in common with modern formal logic in the tradition of Whitehead and Russell's *Principia Mathematica*. It is tempting to draw an analogy between Langland's frequently expressed distrust of the friars' logic and the objections of some modern humanists to the dominance of formal logic and linguistic analysis in contemporary philosophy. The analogy has occurred (though without reference to *Piers Plowman*) to David Knowles, *The English Mystical Tradition* (New York: Harper & Brothers, 1961), p. 42, and to James Crompton in his review of Leff, *Heresy in the Later Middle Ages* (Manchester: Manchester University Press, 1967), *Medium Aevum* 38 (1969):102.

37. Julian of Norwich, *Revelations of Divine Love*, ed. Grace Warrack, 13th ed. (London: Methuen and Co., 1949), pp. 3, 56. On the question of Julian's literacy, see Knowles, *The English Mystical Tradition*, pp. 120–21.

Lift up þin herte vnto God wiþ a meek steryng of loue; &
mene him-self, & none of his goodes. & þerto loke þee loþe to
þenk on ouȝt bot on hym-self, so þat nouȝt worche in þi witte
ne in þi wille bot only him-self. & do þat in þee is to forȝete
alle þe creatures þat euer God maad & þe werkes of hem, so þat
þi þouȝt ne þi desire be not directe ne streche to any of hem,
neiþer in general ne in special. Bot lat hem be, & take no kepe
to hem.

. . . & þerfore schap þee to bide in þis derknes as longe as þou
maist, euermore criing after him þat þou louest; for ȝif euer
shalt þou fele him or see him, as it may be here, it behoueþ
alweis be in þis cloude & in þis derknes.[38]

There is clearly no question here of earth being a "mirror" of God.
It can only be the mirror which Lady Fortune presents to Will. This
whole tendency of thought reveals a despair of reaching God by learning, for as Will puts it, those surest of salvation are "lewed Iuttes"
who "Percen wiþ a Paternoster þe paleys of heuene." But the essential thing to remember about Langland is that this remark of Will's
elicits Scripture's strong rebuke. If Scripture is to be trusted, then
Langland rejects the mystical approach so typical of his day as a way
to salvation.[39]

His reasons for doing so can be gathered from the events and char-
acters of the inner dream. He seems to have seen this mystical exalta-
tion of simplicity as a surrender to indeterminism and skepticism. Because of its purposely weak rational basis, such thinking could all too
easily turn from an emotional commitment to God to an equally emotional libertinism. This is what actually happened in the contemporary
heresy of the "Free Spirit," which Leff links to Ockhamism and to
certain tendencies of the "Rhineland mysticism" of Meister Eckhart
and his school.[40] It is possible Langland had this heresy in mind when
he led Will into his forty-five years of vaguely sketched vice in
the company of Fortune, *Concupiscencia-Carnis*, Coueytise-of-eyes,

38. Phyllis Hodgson, ed., *The Cloud of Unknowing and The Book of Privy
Counselling* (London: Early English Text Society, 1944), pp. 16, 17. I have
omitted some editorial apparatus.

39. A point missed by Maisack, pp. 37–39, who interprets B.X.458ff. as
praise of Cistercian lay brothers.

40. See *Heresy in the Later Middle Ages*, pp. 259–407. The discussion there
restricts itself to Bavaria and the Lowland countries.

Pryde-of-parfyte-lyuynge, and Recklessness. The last-named apostle
of folly cites a poet named Plato in support of his way of life:

> "Ye? recche þee neuere," quod Rechelesnesse, stood forþ in
>   raggede cloþes;
> "Folwe forþ þat Fortune wole; þow hast wel fer til Elde.
> A man may stoupe tyme ynoȝ whan he shal tyne þe crowne."
> "*Homo proponit*," quod a poete, and Plato he hiȝte,
> "And *Deus disponit*," quod he; "lat god doon his wille.
> If truþe wol witnesse it be wel do Fortune to folwe
> *Concupiscencia carnis* ne Coueitise of eiȝes
> Ne shal noȝt greue þee graiþly, ne bigile þee, but þow wolt."
>   (B.XI.34–41)

Here is fourteenth-century voluntarism at its most extreme, and it
could be derived from Bradwardine or Ockham, from the logicians or
the mystics, even though it would not fairly reflect their thought as a
whole. As Langland saw it, their arguments all tended finally to this
equation of the reverent formula "*homo proponit, deus disponit*" with
the less-than-reverent "*carpe diem.*" The very term "truth," whose
dual reference had symbolized a pact of love and intelligibility between God and man, is here used to dissolve the pact. Our rewards
will come at random, because truth itself is random. The C-text puts
it more clearly: "Al that Treuthe a-tacheth and testifieth for goode, /
Thauh thei folwe that Fortune wole, no folie ich hit holde" (C.XII.
306–7). This sounds very much like some remarks of Holkot or Adam
of Woodham in its insistence on the extrinsic, *de jure* connection between man's works and God's rewards.

Having reached this nadir of skepticism, Will begins a process of
recovery, seeking to strike some sort of balance between the power of
God and the freedom of man. With age comes the recognition of the
falseness of Fortune and her friends the friars, and, by the logic of
dreams and of allegories, this recognition is embodied in the sudden
appearance of "Leute." Leute, as we saw in the last chapter, is that
strict regard for human and divine law which forms the social matrix
of love. With love and law he makes up the case, kind, and number
of man's life in its agreement with God's will. Thus he makes sense
only in a world view which sets up an intelligible and certain bond
between man's free acts and God's free response. Like Cacciaguida in

his words to Dante,[41] though with some hedging, Leute tells Will to speak out bravely the hard truths he has learned. Such a commission is an endorsement of the human powers which had so seriously been put in question.

Leute's caution to the dreamer—*"Parum lauda; vitupera parcius"*— is given an odd twist by Scripture, who pops up again and connects it ominously with the text, "Many are called, but few are chosen" (B.XI.112–14; Matt. 22:14). This time the dreamer is able to cope with Scripture's apparent determinism by using his reason and adducing other Scriptural passages to show how God's mercy offers salvation to all. Scripture agrees:

"That is sooþ," seide Scripture; "may no synne lette
Mercy al to amende and Mekenesse hir folwe;
For þei beþ, as oure bokes telleþ, aboue goddes werkes:
Misericordia eius super omnia opera eius."

(B.XI.137–39)[42]

The dreamer wins this argument easily because, instead of simply grasping at texts, he is acting like a learned interpreter of Scripture rather than a passive receiver of it. In so doing he regains some of what he lost in rejecting Clergy.[43]

---

41. *Paradiso* 17.124ff.

42. The Latin text is Ps. 145:9 (Authorized Version).

43. These lines are difficult and can give rise to varying interpretations, of which Wittig's deserves the most careful consideration. He finds in Will's response to Scripture a "false security" based on "the hypothesis that all Christians, once baptized into the life of grace, are saved. The only danger of damnation he sees threaten a Christian is the renunciation of the faith, something he thinks could never occur [lines 125–26]. Will simply relies on man's being saved by reason, conscience, and contrition, no matter how straying and heedless his life" ("Inward Journey," p. 258). There is, first of all, a logical difficulty in the last sentence quoted. A man saved by "reason, conscience, and contrition" (cf. B.XI.131–36) has, by definition, renounced his "straying and heedless . . . life." These agents of salvation are not simply personifications; they are vigorous and decisive movements of the aroused intellect and will. Further, Wittig never deals with Scripture's unequivocal assent to Will's hypothesis—"That is sooþ"—though he does quote it. We certainly must accept Scripture's endorsement. The real difficulty is in the passage beginning line 123, where Langland compares renunciation of faith by a baptized person to the renunciation of a lord's charter by a churl, finding the first as obviously impossible as the second. (For the legal principle involved see *Parallel Texts*, 2:168–69.) The analogy can apply logically only to the "indelible sacramental

Characteristically, the argument swings to the opposite extreme, when Trajan, a good pagan who had been saved, bursts on the scene crying "Ye? baw for bokes!" (B.XI.140) and arguing for the sole sufficiency of good works motivated by love, without Clergy or even the sacraments. Langland's account of Trajan's salvation differs in this from Dante's and from "all known authorities in making Trajan's salvation depend solely upon his own virtues."[44] As R. W. Frank suggests, Langland "clearly altered the Trajan story to illustrate the importance for salvation of good works."[45] The hope Langland expresses here is a rather daring one and has a good deal in common with some of the more optimistic expressions of Ockhamist indeterminism, for instance, with Holkot's assurance that if a man does his very best (*facit quod in se est*), God will respond with the gift of grace, even though He is not absolutely obliged to.[46] To that extent,

character" attributed to baptism (as well as confirmation and ordination), which makes it forever valid and unrepeatable, even for heretics and apostates. (See "Baptême" and "Caractère sacramental" in *Dictionnaire de Théologie Catholique* [Paris: Librairie Letouzey et Ané, 1932], 2:167–378, 1698–1708, esp. 204–6, 1700, 1706.) Will seems to make this character a guarantee of salvation. That is, he seems to make it indistinguishable from grace, which it certainly is not. I cannot help believing that this represents a wish just short of conviction on the part of Langland himself (cf. B.XVIII.371–72, 377–78), but it is possible to read Will's lines as a somewhat imprecise statement of a more orthodox position. Scripture's first text ("*Multi enim sunt vocati; pauci vero electi*," Matt. 22:14) seems to state a categorical exclusion of many from salvation. Will's response points to the strong possibility, if not the certainty, of their acceptance. The role of man's will and works is specified, though perhaps with insufficient emphasis (cf. 119, 131–36). Will stresses instead the guarantee of baptism, which is offered to all (114), that he *is not excluded*. Scripture's assent is specifically directed to this negative guarantee: ". . . may no synne lette / Mercy al to amende and Mekenesse hir folwe" (138). That last conditional clause brings the human responsibility into somewhat sharper relief than Will had done, but this is an adjustment of emphasis within a general assent to the substance of Will's statement.

44. R. W. Chambers, "Long Will, Dante, and the Righteous Heathen," in *Essays and Studies by Members of the English Association*, 9 (Oxford: Oxford University Press, 1924):66. Dante's account of Trajan's salvation is in *Paradiso* 20.106ff. T. P. Dunning, in "Langland and the Salvation of the Heathen," *Medium Aevum* 12 (1943):45–54, argues for Langland's general orthodoxy on this point. R. W. Frank, *Salvation*, pp. 60ff., maintains Chambers's view. It seems to me that regardless of his real orthodoxy or heterodoxy Langland felt as though he were going out on a limb for the righteous heathen.

45. Frank, *Salvation*, p. 61. Cf. Wittig, pp. 249–55.

46. See Heiko Augustinus Oberman, *The Harvest of Medieval Theology: Gabriel Biel and Late Medieval Nominalism* (Cambridge: Harvard University Press, 1963), pp. 235–48, esp. 246. Oberman argues throughout his work that Leff and others have laid too much stress on the skeptical elements in the thought of the Ockhamists.

Langland is himself an Ockhamist: he will subscribe to indeterminism as long as it opens doors to salvation.

He develops his position in a long speech which finally wobbles out of control and which, in B, is not clearly assigned to anyone.[47] Trajan, we are told, attributes his salvation to his adherence to the law of love which he, like Study, calls a "leel science" transcending all others (B.XI.167, 171–72). Rather quickly, Langland identifies the law of love with the ideal of patient poverty, which in Passus XIII will be embodied in the riddling Patience. Patient poverty is the good life (or "Dowel") in its essence, but not everyone is called to it. Some, like Trajan himself in history and legend, will follow less perfect lives which gain their legitimacy from care and love for the patient poor,[48] who are types of Christ in this world:

> For oure Ioye and oure Iuel, Iesu crist of heuene,
> In a pouere mannes apparaille pursueþ vs euere,
> And lokeþ on vs in hir liknesse and þat wiþ louely chere
> To knowen vs by oure kynde herte and castynge of oure eiȝen,
> Wheiþer we loue þe lordes here bifore þe lord of blisse;
>
> . . . .
>
> Why I meue þis matere is moost for þe pouere;
> For in hir liknesse oure lord lome haþ ben yknowe.
> Witnesse in þe Pask wyke, whan he yede to Emaus;
>
> . . . .
>
> And in þe apparaille of a pouere man and pilgrymes liknesse
> Many tyme god haþ ben met among nedy peple,
> Ther neuere segge hym seiȝ in secte of þe riche.
>
> (B.XI.185–89, 232–34, 243–45)

Langland circles back obsessively to this scene of recognition, where the figure of Christ Himself on earth assures us that heaven and earth are still bound together as they were in the Incarnation. We see this bond in human good works which define themselves as such by their

47. Skeat attributes the speech to Leute, but with no clear justification, in *Parallel Texts*, 2:169; Donaldson suggests that Will himself is the speaker, in *C-Text*, pp. 173–74; Kirk, *Dream Thought*, p. 136, suggests Scripture, or, just possibly, Trajan. The C-text gives the speech to Recklessness.

48. Dante, in *Purgatorio* 10.73–96, alludes to a widely known story of Trajan's gracious assistance to a poor widow and makes him a type of the virtue of humility. This episode aroused Gregory to his prayers for Trajan's salvation. See Wittig for an account of the tradition (pp. 249–55).

relation to patient poverty. Our surprised encounters with the very face of Christ watching us with loving concern refute the disjunctions of the Ockhamists. There is a real connection between God and his creatures, between God's free will and man's. It is not proven by logical argumentation but by the sudden glimpse of a face in the crowd, often the face of a poor man, sometimes the face of an honest plowman.

By the end of Passus XI, then, Will once more begins to come to terms with the world as reflection of the divine Idea. Though it may be difficult to remember after so much digression and confusion, the passage in which he does so recalls the speech of Wit in Passus IX:

> And slepynge I seiȝ al þis, and siþen cam kynde
> And nempned me by my name and bad me nymen hede,
> And þoruȝ þe wondres of þis world wit for to take.
> And on a mountaigne þat myddelerþe hiȝte, as me þo þouȝte,
> I was fet forþ by forbisenes to knowe
> Thorugh ech a creature kynde my creatour to louye.
>
> (B.XI.321–26)[49]

To call God "Kynde" as Wit had done is to speak of Him as intelligible through the order of nature which He has created. The point is made even more precisely in the C-text where "Myddel-erde" is not a mountain but a mirror:

> Thus Rechelessnesse in a rage a-resonede clergie,
> And scornede Scripture that meny skyles shewede,
> Til that Kynde cam Clergie to helpen,
> And in the myrour of Myddel-erde made hym eft to loke,
> To knowe by ech creature Kynde to louye.
>
> (C.XIV.129–33)[50]

It is, in fact, the very mirror Dame Fortune offered to Will, but perhaps now it is being held at a different angle. Once Will gets over his petulant rage with Clergy and Scripture the world as mirror regains

---

49. In Skeat the last line (his line 317) reads: "Thorugh eche a creature and Kynde my creatoure to louye." Kane and Donaldson's reading, by eliminating "and," significantly alters syntax and sense.

50. The protagonist in this part of the C-text is not the Dreamer but Recklessness, in a much expanded role. See Donaldson, *C-Text*, pp. 171ff.

its proper function. Here, more clearly than anywhere else, Langland rejects the mystical way to God by forgetfulness of His creatures. His God is named "Kynde" and we reach Him by "a kynde knowing."

The reappearance of Reason shows further this healing of the breach between God and creation. Reason has a dual aspect in medieval thought. On the one hand it is the power of the individual rational intellect. On the other, it is the transcendent order by which God created the world. It is in this aspect that it appears as the quasi-angelic *Ratio* governing creation. His very appearance asserts an ultimate harmony between the order of the mind and the order of creation and heals the incisions of Ockham's razor, conferring at once a value and a limitation on the workings of man's intellect. The value is to be found in the intellectual discovery of order, a discovery which retraces creation to the Wisdom which is our mind's exemplar. The limitation is placed on our inquiries into why God ordered things in such a way. To do this is to substitute contingency for what had seemed a necessary order, and to threaten the intelligibility of creation and its link to God. This was the irreverence of Ockhamism, and it is the fault of Will in his exchange with Reason. He questions one specific point in the order of creation, why Reason does not govern men as infallibly as he governs beasts. Langland apparently considered this part of a more general questioning, because in the next Passus Imaginatif rebukes the dreamer for having asked Reason why flowers have certain colors, why different kinds of birds build certain kinds of nests, and so on (B.XII.217ff.). To ask such questions, which cannot be answered by our reasons as such but require empirical investigation, is really to call into doubt the existence of Reason as a stable, objective entity, as a divine idea corresponding to our subjective reason and securing its stability. It is to wield Ockham's razor once again.

The specific question raised by the dreamer, why Reason does not govern men as surely as he does beasts, is a commonplace in discussions of the order of Nature. It is raised, for example, in the popular work of Alain de Lille, *De Planctu Naturae.*[51] Reason's answer is that such governance is possible to God, but its time is not yet. God knows when its time will come and, in the meanwhile, puts up with man's waywardness. Our duty in response is to follow the example of

---

51. Nature's complaint here, like Will's, has to do with sexual excesses, though mainly those of sodomy. See *De planctu naturae* (*PL* 210:448–50), a notable instance of grammatical metaphor.

His patience in our inquiries, like Reason himself who, in his first appearance (B.IV.20), rode a horse named "suffre-til-I-se-my-tyme." In the present state of things, Reason, as the law of God, governs animals, plants, and inanimate nature, those parts of nature which do not have reason in themselves. Through Reason, Kind "is þe pies patron and putteþ it in hir ere / That þere þe þorn is þikkest to buylden and brede" (B.XII.227–28). If God governed man in the same way, we would be right back in Bradwardine's determinist universe where God is "senior partner" in all acts of our wills. Will's impetuous demand for hard and final answers threatens to drive him into the very predestinarianism that had chilled his heart in Passus X. Reason does not govern men as it does animals because it is man's internal possession as well as his external norm. Man is free, and thus capable of sin and of the love that saved Trajan and that finds the face of Christ among the patient poor. The time is still to come when reason as internal faculty and Reason as transcendent norm will coincide. Their coincidence will be accompanied by others, between the individual and social conscience, between leute and law, between the king in his Body Natural and in his Body Politic. In the meantime, until that ideal order is realized, Kind "draws an example of it externally, so that what was known only to him may be seen plainly by others" in the order of Nature.[52]

We shall not move beyond this by our own powers. When we try to do so, as the inquisitive dreamer does, we irreverently question the order established by God. When we have learned that order, when we see through it the objective norm of Reason, then we can only follow Reason's counsel to wait patiently for God's next gesture toward His creation. It is at this point that Truth becomes Love, as it did in Lady Holy Church's speech. When the dreamer resumes his progress toward the vision of the Redemption his guide will be Patience and his companion will be Conscience, whom we have not seen since the opening scenes in the king's court. Having gained the humility and sufferance which are the final fruits of intellectualism the dreamer can struggle forward into the regions that seemed so misty to Study. His last guides will be those of Theology, specifically the three theological virtues of Faith, Hope, and Charity, which last turns out to be Piers and Christ Himself. We know that the dreamer is ready for this next stage of the journey when he tells Imaginatif, with-

52. Hugh of Saint Victor, *The Didascalicon*, p. 156.

out coaching, what Do-well is: "To se muche and suffre moore, certes, is dowel" (B.XI.412). Such sufferance is both individual and social, awaiting the salvation of the soul and the apocalyptic reformation of the world to the image of God. It is the counsel of Reason in both his aspects, and it will soon be personified in Patience.

Imaginatif, whose conversation with Will in Passus XII has such pivotal importance in the poem, is a very difficult faculty to define. Medieval thought gives the *vis imaginativa* a rather lowly role as an "internal sense" collecting and coordinating sense impressions. In some accounts it has a sort of rudimentary "calculative and deliberative" function, suggesting the pleasure or pain likely to arise from the objects of the senses.[53] It could thus be related to the virtue of prudence as Langland's character seems to be when he recounts his services to the dreamer:

> I haue folwed þee, in feiþ, þise fyue and fourty wynter,
> And manye tymes haue meued þee to mynne on þyn ende,
> And how fele fernyeres are faren and so fewe to come;
> And of þi wilde wantownesse whiles þow yong were
> To amende it in þi myddel age, lest myȝt þe faille
> In þyn olde elde, þat yuele kan suffre
> Pouerte or penaunce, or preyeres bidde.
>
> (B.XII.3–9)[54]

Morton Bloomfield notes "that 'imaginatif' in any medieval psychological system would be responsible for dreams," so that "It would be proper . . . for the putative source of the dreams Will was dreaming to be his instructor, for it was imagination (as an internal sense) which gave him the framework of his poem."[55] I think that this can

53. See H. S. V. Jones, "Imaginatif in Piers Plowman," *Journal of English and Germanic Philology* 13 (1914):583–88; Randolph Quirk, "Vis Imaginativa," ibid. 53 (1954):81–83; Wittig, "Inward Journey," pp. 271–72; and "Imaginatif," 2 a, b, c, in *Middle English Dictionary*, ed. H. Kurath et al. (Ann Arbor: University of Michigan Press, 1954–).

54. Langland consistently uses "imagine" with its common ME connotation of prudential judgment, whether moral or immoral; cf. B.XIII.357–59; XIX.276–78; XX.31–34.

55. *Apocalypse*, p. 172. Bloomfield also suggests that Langland may have been influenced by treatments of imagination as a prophetic faculty in Arabic and Jewish philosophy. Dante's "alta fantasia" (*Paradiso* 33.142) seems to reflect some such heightening of the faculty's position. In the case of Imaginatif,

be made more specific. Imaginatif claims responsibility not for all the dreams in the poem (though he might), but for the inner dream which has just concluded. He says he has followed the dreamer "þise fyue and fourty wynter," and near the beginning of the inner dream Will tells us that "Coueitise of eiȝes . . . folwed me fourty wynter and a fifte moore" (B.XI.46, 47). This limitation of his scope of action is understandable since he himself is appearing in a dream, as we are reminded at the end of his speech when the dreamer "awaked þerwiþ" (B.XIII.1).[56]

Joseph Wittig calls attention to the adjectival form of the character's name, "Imaginatif" rather than "Imaginacioun," finding in it "a clear tendency . . . to refer, not to one limited faculty, but to a more inclusive activity one might describe as 'representing vividly to oneself.' . . . Excited to a personal confrontation of his culpability and possible damnation and moved by the emotions of fear and shame experienced in Passus 11, the dreamer becomes attentive and concerned about the thought of his own end, becomes in fact 'imaginatif.' "[57]

Imaginatif's advice to the dreamer is remarkable for the way it reduces the highly abstract issues of the inner dream to common sense judgments; and he does this without losing sight of the larger mysteries that his counsels imply. Like a popular preacher, he handles Scripture with a sometimes loose regard for the principal intent of the letter in order to make a point about the practical facts of moral life. One of his more important points, the value of good works and the salvation of the righteous heathen, is based on a rather slanted reading of 1 Peter 4:18:

> "*Contra!*" quod Ymaginatif þoo and comsed to loure,
> And seide, "*Saluabitur vix Iustus in die Iudicij*;
> *Ergo saluabitur*," quod he and seide na moore latyn.
>   (B.XII.280–82)

---

though, this seems to me a little more than the text will bear. Perhaps we should follow Wittig's suggestion (pp. 273–74) that the assumption that Imaginatif's role is "exalted" is unwarranted and leads to false problems in identifying him.

56. The connection between the two lines seems confirmed by the careful omission of both references to forty-five years in the C-text. Apparently this is autobiographical and does not fit Recklessness, who replaces the dreamer in C. Cf. C.XIII.1ff., and C.XV.1ff.

57. "Inward Journey," pp. 272, 274.

Such sleights of hand paradoxically show a great respect for Scripture. As the word of God, Scripture is polysemous, and so our choice of meanings is not governed by the letter but by a prudential judgment about what will best conduce to our reunion with the word's Source.

The salvation of the just heathen has a direct bearing on the value of learning or Clergy because here, as in the earlier dispute with Scripture, the problem is felt most poignantly in the cases of men like Aristotle and Socrates. Men are saved, finally, by grace. Is there any direct relationship of learning to grace? The doctrinal heart of Imaginatif's speech addresses itself to this question and informs all his practical advice. First he seems to make wisdom as much a liability as riches:

> "Sapience, seiþ þe bok, swelleþ a mannes soule:
> *Sapiencia inflat & c*;
> And Richesse riȝt so but if þe roote be trewe.
> Ac grace is a gras þerfor þo greuaunces to abate.
> Ac grace ne groweþ noȝt til good wil yeve reyn;
> Pacience and pouerte þe place is þer it groweþ,
> And in lele lyuynge men and in lif holy,
> And þoruȝ þe gifte of þe holy goost as þe gospel telleþ:
> *Spiritus vbi vult spirat*."
>
> (B.XII.57–63)[58]

This tends in the direction of Scripture's counsel to Will, with its scorn of riches and of the institutions that live on riches. But it is not quite so uncompromising. Riches can be a benefit if "þe roote be trewe," and grace is a "gras," a healing herb that can purge riches of their evils. A social economy of grace seems to be implicit in the lines about patient poverty, for it is among the patient poor that the grace (gras) grows that will heal the rich. So if riches can be rendered innocuous or even beneficial for men's salvation it is because of the grace whose proper home is among the poor. We have here the outlines of a society based on mutual love and tending toward a kind of corporate salvation.

The redemption of Wisdom begins in much the same way but is carried a good deal further:

---

58. The Latin texts are 1 Cor. 8:1 and John 3.8.

"Clergie and kynde wit comeþ of siȝte and techyng
As þe book bereþ witnesse to burnes þat kan rede:
Quod scimus loquimur, quod vidimus testamur.
Of *quod scimus* comeþ Clergie, a konnynge of heuene,
And of *quod vidimus* comeþ kynde wit, of siȝte of diuerse peple.
Ac grace is a gifte of god and of greet loue spryngeþ;
Knew neuere clerk how it comeþ forþ, ne kynde wit þe weyes:
Nescit aliquis vnde venit aut quo vadit & c.
Ac yet is Clergie to comende and kynde wit boþe,
And namely Clergie for cristes loue, þat of Clergie is roote."
(B.XII.64–71)[59]

Learning cannot win or even explain God's free gift of grace, and yet learning has Christ as its root, Christ who is also the source of grace. If their source is the same, then grace and learning must have some kind of direct relationship. It seems that learning, if not a cause of grace, is yet a figure or symbol of it. The two are parallel emanations from Christ, meeting at infinity, in that area of mystery where Study's eyesight failed, where she could only take Theology's word for it that the root and final cause of all her endeavor is Love.

Imaginatif proves this relation between learning and grace by some curious readings of Scripture: since God wrote the commandments, and since Christ comforted the woman taken in adultery and damned those who would stone her by writing their sins in the sand, therefore writing and learning are blessed and endorsed by the Son of God. He then gives the second example a rather surprising development, moving the discussion into the area of mystery where learning and grace converge:

"So clergie is confort to creatures þat repenten,
And to mansede men meschief at hire ende.
For goddes body myȝte noȝt ben of breed wiþouten clergie,
The which body is boþe boote to þe riȝtfulle
And deeþ and dampnacion to hem þat deyeþ yuele,
As cristes carectes confortede, and boþe coupable shewed
The womman þat þe Iewes iugged þat Iesus þouȝte to saue:
Nolite iudicare & non iudicabimini.
Riȝt so goddes body, breþeren, but it be worþili taken,

59. The Latin texts are John 3:11 and 8.

Dampneþ vs at þe day of dome as dide þe carectes þe Iewes.
Forþi I counseille þee for cristes sake clergie þat þow louye;
For kynde wit is of his kyn and neiȝe Cosynes boþe
To oure lord, leue me; forþi loue hem, I rede.
For boþe ben as Mirours to amenden by defautes
And lederes for lewed men and for lettred boþe.
Forþi lakke þow neuere logik, lawe ne his custumes,
Ne countreplede clerkes, I counseille þee for euere."

(B.XII.83–98)[60]

We have here a near equation of Christ's written word which represents learning, and Christ's body which, in the Eucharist, is the continuing presence in the world of the grace of the Incarnation. This is
the most radical statement of the sacramental, priestly character of
Clergy. It stands behind all the more logical, common sense arguments of Imaginatif about how learning shows us the way to salvation, how a learned man knows how to make a perfect act of contrition, the example of the two men in the Thames, and so on. Learning,
including even logic, is a cousin of Christ. Learning's misuse does not
destroy this relationship, any more than an unworthy reception of the
Eucharist invalidates its sacramental character; instead, in both cases,
the offense is raised to sacrilege because it deals with holy things.
Learning is the result of divine illumination which is "after þe grace
of god." As we learned from Saint Bonaventure, the activities of the
mind in the service of learning differ from the workings of grace in
our progress to salvation only as an image differs from a likeness.[61]

Some further, general similarities can be noted between Langland's
procedure with Imaginatif and that of Hugh of Saint Victor and Saint
Bonaventure in linking learning to grace. Hugh said that the final end
of all learning was "to restore within us the divine likeness, a likeness
which to us is a form but to God is his nature." Saint Bonaventure
adopted Hugh's grouping of the arts and showed in detail how each
of them reveals the image of God in the Trinity and the image of
man's relation to God. The title of his treatise, *Retracing the Arts to
Theology*, suggests Langland's project and the uncomprehending but
sincere respect of Study for the science that "leteþ best bi loue." Saint
Bonaventure's *reductio* proceeds mainly by way of metaphor and

60. The Latin text is Matt. 7:1.
61. The sacramental connotations of learning are strongly suggested in the
following lines, through XII.158.

symbol, discerning structural analogies between the pursuit of divine truth in theology and the pursuit of the secular truths proper to each of the liberal and mechanical arts. He even finds a fourfold meaning in each art which corresponds to the fourfold meaning that theologians found in Scripture. This suggests the procedure of Imaginatif when he makes Christ's "caractes" a type of learning and then of Christ's very body in the Eucharist. It also suggests Langland's procedure later when he makes the transition from the intellectual sufferance counseled by Imaginatif to the more specifically moral virtue personified in Patience. The first is a figure of the second. Saint Bonaventure might say that Patience is the "pattern of life" adumbrated tropologically by our entertaining the difficulties and apparent contradictions of our studies.

When Conscience takes his courteous leave of Clergy, in the poem's nearest equivalent to the parting of Dante and Vergil on the threshold of Paradise, he indicates such a transitional role for Patience: " 'If Pacience be oure partyng felawe and pryue with vs boþe / Ther nys wo in þis world þat we ne sholde amende' " (B.XIII.206–7). Patience himself, in the B-text, indicates this by proposing a riddle as the answer to the question about Do-well, Do-bet, and Do-best.[62] A riddle addresses itself specifically to the intellect and challenges it to move beyond itself into the new simplicity where the patient acceptance of faith will be the rule. Significantly, when the C-text omits the riddle, it introduces a new challenge by the sudden, irrational intrusion of Piers, who will soon become the human nature of Christ, the central riddle of Christianity (C.XVI.138–50). Each of these surprising developments is a consequence of the life of learning which learning itself cannot account for. Each reveals a new aspect of its true, symbolic character. Thus it is that the last personification we meet before we enter the transparent simplicity of the vision of the Redemption is Anima, the human soul in the most inclusive sense, revealing itself in its varied action as *Anima, Animus, Mens, Racio, Sensus*, Conscience, *Amor*, and *Spiritus* (B.XV.23–36).[63] All the

62. B.XIII.135–56. The riddle is gradually being deciphered. See Ben H. Smith, "Patience's Riddle, Piers Plowman, B, XIII," *Modern Language Notes* 76 (1961):675–82; R. E. Kaske, "*Ex Vi Transicionis* and Its Passage in *Piers Plowman*," *Journal of English and Germanic Philology* 62 (1963):32–60; and Edward G. Schweitzer, " 'Half a Laumpe Lyne in Latyne' and Patience's Riddle in *Piers Plowman*," ibid. 73 (1974):313–27.

63. As Langland notes (1. 37), the source of this description of Anima is Isidore of Seville. See Skeat's note in *Parallel Texts*, 2:215.

mental faculties converge in this figure. All their different illuminations return to him like colored rays to a prism, to emerge in the
simple white light of Scripture, the story of the Redemption which
breaks into Passus XVI, when Piers shakes the Tree of Charity
"Amyddes mannes body." The image of God and of the Redemption
are generated by the soul in action as it searches for God and its own
salvation. The *Vita de Dowel* is thus a massive demonstration of the
principles laid down in the speech of Lady Holy Church. The search
for truth, in this instance through the life of learning, is eventually
its own reward. Truth in the end is neither a fixed object nor a set
answer to a question but the soul's measured movement of love which
imitates and invokes divine Wisdom and which constitutes the real
relation of man to his Creator.

5. The Pardon, Piers, and Christ

I HAVE RESERVED until the last a full treatment of those questions which probably occur first to any reader of *Piers Plowman*, namely: who or what is this elusive character who gives his name to the poem; and what is the meaning of the scene in which he tears the pardon sent by Truth and argues with the priest? These questions lie at the poem's heart and have elicited some of the best criticism it has received. My own answers build upon the best of this criticism, and in them I shall try to bring to a focus the issues raised in my earlier chapters.

We shall begin with the pardon scene because it is a smaller, more stable entity than Piers himself. To do this, though, we must give a provisional identification of the scene's protagonist and thus anticipate our treatment of the second problem. Suffice it to say, for the moment, that Piers is a man of simple goodness who is unique in knowing the way to Truth. His authority is therefore more binding than any which society confers upon its official rulers and teachers. We see this most clearly when, later in the poem, Piers turns up once again as the human nature of Christ. In his first appearance, though, there are only vague hints of this.[1] He emerges suddenly from the midst of a repentant crowd, who, after the confessions of the Deadly Sins, "Cride vpward to Crist and to his clene moder / To haue grace

1. Kirk, pp. 9–13, comments on the need to respond to the poem "linearly," to respond to its allegorical content as it unfolds, and thus, for example, not to insist on Piers's allegorical significances too early.

to go to truþe, God leue þat þei moten" (B.V.511–12). Piers tells them he knows the way and he describes the path that leads there, through the Ten Commandments, Penance, Grace, and into the court of Truth "in þyn herte" (B.V.606). Before leading them there, however, he must work his half acre, and they must work to help him. A small society begins to take shape here, with Piers assigning to a knight the task of protecting him and his like in return for their obedient service (B.VI.21–56). Piers draws up a will which epitomizes the good Christian life in society (B.VI.83–104), but then finds this ideal being violated by loafers who defy him and the knight. He calls in Hunger, whose discipline of the workers is a prompt but only temporary solution. It is at this point that Truth, God, intervenes:

> Treuþe herde telle herof, and to Piers sente
> To taken his teme and tilien þe erþe,
> And purchaced hym a pardoun *a pena & a culpa*
> For hym and for hise heires eueremoore after.
> And bad hym holde hym at home and erien hise leyes,
> And alle þat holpen to erye or to sowe,
> Or any maner mestier þat myჳte Piers helpe,
> Pardon wiþ Piers Plowman truþe haþ ygraunted.
>
> (B.VII.1–8)[2]

A long passage follows describing what share different groups in society have in this pardon and constituting an encyclopedic social criticism.

The crucial episode, much of which is missing from the C-text, begins with the entrance of a priest who offers to interpret the pardon:

> "Piers," quod a preest þoo, "þi pardon moste I rede,
> For I shal construe ech clause and kenne it þee on englissh."
> And Piers at his preiere þe pardon vnfoldeþ,
> And I bihynde hem boþe biheld al þe bulle.
> In two lynes it lay and noჳt a lettre moore,
> And was writen riჳt þus in witnesse of truþe:

2. The last half-line reads "þe pope haþ hem grauntid" in A.VIII.8, and "perpetual he graunteth" in C.X.8. Apparently Langland wanted to refrain from so emphatic an endorsement of the Pope, whose pardons he distrusted, and yet wanted the richer alliteration he had to forego in B. See Nevill Coghill, "The Pardon of Piers Plowman," *Proceedings of the British Academy* 30 (1944):318–20.

Et qui bona egerunt ibunt in vitam eternam;
Qui vero mala in ignem eternum.
"Peter!" quod þe preest þoo, "I kan no pardon fynde
But do wel and haue wel, and god shal haue þi soule,
And do yuel and haue yuel, and hope þow noon ooþer
That after þi deeþ day þe deuel shal haue þi soule."
And Piers for pure tene pulled it asonder
And seide, "*Si ambulauero in medio vmbre mortis*
Non timebo mala quoniam tu mecum es.
I shal cessen of my sowyng," quod Piers, "& swynke noȝt so
    harde,
Ne aboute my bilyue so bisy be na moore;
Of preieres and of penaunce my plouȝ shal ben herafter,
And wepen whan I sholde werche þouȝ whete breed me faille."

(B.VII.107–25)

This dramatic interchange is one of the most enigmatic passages in
the poem. What are we to make of a pardon from Truth which simply
contains the last two lines of the Athanasian Creed? Why does Piers
tear it? Is he rejecting it? And if so, why? Or is he angry at himself?
What relevance do the psalm and Piers's commentary on it have to
his anger and to the pardon?

In general, the most satisfactory answers to these questions, have
been those offered by Robert W. Frank who argues, against most
previous critics, that Piers's anger is directed at the priest, and that
his tearing of the pardon does not signify his rejection of it, though he
and Will share a distrust of pardons from Rome. Frank points out
that this pardon is a rather special sort of document, actually an anti-
pardon: "Just as Piers' Testament is not really a will but a device for
communicating an ethical message dramatically by means of the con-
trast between the conventional form and its novel content, so too the
pardon is not really an orthodox pardon but a device for stating an
ethical principle dramatically. The clash between form and content
is even sharper here, for this pardon contains a message which is by
implication an attack on pardons and which does in fact lead to such
an attack by the Dreamer. How, then, can we speak of it as we would
of a conventional pardon, as a piece of parchment, a bull with seals.
That is precisely what it is not. In accepting its message, Piers is rejecting bulls with seals. In tearing the parchment, Piers is symboli-

cally tearing paper pardons from Rome."[3] As Frank admits, the tearing of the pardon remains "a very confusing sign" even after his explanation, and this is probably one reason why the C-text omits it.

Howard Meroney makes a suggestion which modifies a detail of Frank's reading and, I think, clarifies some of the scene's emotional content. He suggests that one of Piers's prototypes in this scene is Moses, for "his people, unawed by famine, sing 'trollilolli!' when they should toil, like the stiff-necked tribe who danced in the wilderness of Sinai." The pardon is "a brief Decalogue" and its rejection by the priest prompts Piers to tear it "even as Moses in wrath broke apart the Tablets of the Law."[4] So Piers's tearing of the pardon is no more a rejection of it than the action of Moses was a rejection of the Ten Commandments. If Moses' receipt of the Ten Commandments should be present to our minds as we read the pardon scene, so too should its fulfillment in the Redemption. For one thing, the word *pardon* suggests this. For another, we are told that "Treuth . . . *purchaced* hym a pardoun*," which implies that there was a price for God to pay. So the pardon scene presents to us the Old Testament "figure"[5] and its fulfillment, the decalogue of Moses and the Redemption, superimposed one upon the other.

Once we see this connection with the Redemption and its Old Testament prefigurations, we may see connections with some other parts of the poem. These, in turn, will enlarge our understanding of the two Latin lines from the Athanasian Creed whose meaning seemed all too commonplace to the priest. Such a message, as he read it, could hardly have the quasi-sacramental force of a pardon. But here, as in the speech of Lady Holy Church, the ordinary moral law is given more than its natural meaning. Its supernatural efficacy through grace gives it the character of a mystery. In both passages the operative word is "truth" and, in both, the transformation of man's natural

3. Frank, *Salvation*, p. 28. An earlier version of Frank's arguments is "The Pardon Scene in *Piers Plowman*," *Speculum* 26 (1951):317–31.

4. Howard Meroney, "The Life and Death of Longe Wille," *ELH* 17 (1950):18. Carruthers, *Search for Saint Truth*, pp. 70–73, notes the same parallel and adduces the "exegetical tradition" that "makes the breaking of the tablets . . . a type of the change from the Old Law to the New." Her application of this to Langland seems to me a little forced. It has some affinities with the study of Rosemary Woolf, cited below.

5. On the special meaning of this term see Erich Auerbach, "Figura," trans. Ralph Manheim, in *Scenes from the Drama of European Literature* (New York: Meridian Books, 1959), pp. 11–76.

good works into supernatural acts is accomplished through the medium of the Incarnation and Redemption. Looking back to Lady Holy Church's speech we find that the impulse to good works was one with the movement by which God became man, when Love who is His Son "hadde of þe erthe yeten hitselue" (B.I.142–54). Her description of "truth" places the origins of the moral law in mystery. When Piers receives the pardon from Truth in its transcendent aspect as God Himself, the commonplace moral message is given its higher meaning. Man's good works are given the divine endorsement which followed upon the Incarnation. Piers's anger at the priest can be compared to Lady Holy Church's impatience with the dreamer. Just as the dreamer seemed to want an explanation of "truth" which would bypass the day-to-day morality which is the human term of the mystery, so the priest wants a pardon which is in itself a talisman of grace instead of a direction to it through good works. To find one of her priests at odds with Lady Holy Church herself would be enough to drive any honest plowman to "pure tene."

I should note that such an interpretation of the pardon's meaning is at odds with that given in some of the best recent accounts of the scene. These have in common a tendency to read the pardon's two lines as a stern and frightening statement of God's justice, which reminds Piers and us of our radical dependence on His countervailing mercy. In the manner of Paul's Epistle to the Romans, it points to the gulf between man and God and to the impossibility of man's meeting God's standards without a free condescension on His part to our inadequacy. Such readings place a heavy emphasis on the threat of damnation in the second line.[6] My own interpretation would take the Epistle General of James, with its emphasis on the need for good works (and hence on their efficacy) in the scheme of salvation, as the more relevant gloss. I also would place the greater emphasis on the first line of the pardon. After all, the threat of damnation is no news. It is the natural fate of all men since the Fall, even of those who have "done well" by their lights. What is new is the access of grace which makes good works supernaturally effective, which brings good men to

6. Three such studies are John Lawlor, "Piers Plowman: The Pardon Reconsidered," *Modern Language Review* 45 (1950):449–58; Rosemary Woolf, "The Tearing of the Pardon," in S. S. Hussey, ed., *Piers Plowman: Critical Approaches* (London: Methuen, 1969), pp. 50–75; and Kirk, *Dream Thought*, pp. 80–100. Each develops a substantial and complex interpretation and deserves a careful reading.

heaven. The pardon's main effect, therefore, is to give human goodness a power it does not have of itself, and to offer an extraordinary
incentive to the fulfillment of ordinary duties on Piers's half-acre, if
only the workers will heed it, and if only the priest will promulgate it.

So Langland sees in the pardon a divine endorsement of good
works, and, as his poem develops, he tries to extend this endorsement
even to the unbaptized. Thus we are told that Trajan was saved
"Nouȝt þoruȝ preiere of a pope but for his pure truþe" (B.XI.156).
In Trajan's words,

> "clerkes wite þe soþe
> That al þe clergie vnder crist ne myȝte me cracche fro helle,
> But oonliche loue and leautee and my laweful domes.
> Gregorie wiste þis wel, and wilned to my soule
> Sauacion for sooþnesse þat he seiȝ in my werkes."
>
> (B.XI.143–47)

Trajan invokes love, law, and leute, which, in Conscience's grammatical metaphor in the C-text, are refracted through the Incarnation to
become the kind, number, and case that harmonize our lives with the
order of heaven. As the unidentified speaker of Passus XI elaborates
on the example of Trajan, he constructs a sort of underground connection between his good deeds and the Redemption:

> "Loue and lewtee is a leel science,
> For þat is þe book blissed of blisse and of ioye;
> God wrouȝte it and wroot it wiþ his owene fynger,
> And took it moises vpon þe mount alle men to lere."
>
> (B.XI.167–70)

In Lady Holy Church's speech on truth, the transition to truth as Love
or Christ is marked by a similar mention of Moses, to whom God
taught love as "þe leueste þyng and moost lik to heuene" (B.I.151).
And, as we just saw, there seems to be a conflation of Moses' reception of the Commandments and the Redemption in the pardon episode. The commentator on Trajan's salvation seems to be moving
toward a similar conflation here. When he finally turns explicitly to
the Redemption, he speaks in terms that recall Piers's concern before
the pardon came for his "blody breþeren for god bouȝte vs alle"
(B.VI.207):

"For alle are we cristes creatures and of his cofres riche,
And breþeren as of oo blood, as wel beggeres as Erles.
For at Caluarie of cristes blood cristendom gan sprynge,
And blody breþeren we bicome þere of o body ywonne.

. . . .

In þe olde lawe, as þe lettre telleþ, mennes sones men called vs
Of Adames issue and Eue ay til god man deide;
And after his resurexcion *Redemptor* was his name,
And we hise breþeren þoruȝ hym ybouȝt, boþe riche and
   pouere."

(B.XI.199–202, 205–8)

It seems from this passage that the new fatherhood of Christ is no less inclusive than the old fatherhood of Adam, and that the good works even of the unbaptized are consecrated in the pardon purchased by Truth.

This is the argument of Imaginatif when he maintains, against the dreamer, that a righteous heathen like Trajan can be saved. His remarkable gloss on "*saluabitur vix iustus in die iudicij,*" which we discussed in the previous chapter, has as its main point the supernatural efficacy of "truth":

"Ne wolde neuere trewe god but trewe truþe were allowed.
And wheiþer it worþ of truþe or noȝt, þe worþ of bileue is gret,
And an hope hangynge þerInne to haue a mede for his truþe;
For *Deus dicitur quasi dans eternam vitam suis, hoc est
   fidelibus;*
   Et alibi, si ambulauero in medio vmbre mortis.
The glose graunteþ vpon þat vers a greet mede to truþe."

(B.XII.290–94)[7]

Imaginatif here returns to the verse to which Piers appealed when the priest impugned his pardon, and he uses it in just the same way, as

7. I have not been able to find the source of the Latin line before Ps. 23:4. The gloss referred to by Imaginatif is probably that of Saint Augustine: ". . . for even if I walk in the midst of this life, which is the shadow of death, . . . I will not fear evils because you dwell in my heart through faith; and now are you with me, so that after the shadow of death I may also be with you." *Enarrationes in Psalmos,* in *PL* 36:182; followed closely, in part verbatim, by the *Glossa Ordinaria,* ibid. 113:876, and Peter Lombard, *Commentarius in Psalmos Davidicos,* ibid. 191:243.

an expression of hope in the supernatural efficacy conferred by God's mercy on the good works of a righteous man, an efficacy which His ordained ministers questioned, finding no pardon in the injunction simply to do well. These lines at the end of Passus XII gather many of the poem's leading motifs thus far, uniting the key terms *truþe* and *mede* with Piers's consoling psalm.

By introducing the new term *hope* the passage also anticipates one of the dreamer's last instructors as he approaches the vision of the Redemption. Hope is personified in Moses, rushing to Jerusalem:

> "I am *Spes*, a spie," quod he, "and spire after a Knyght
> That took me a maundement vpon þe mount of Synay
> To rule alle Reames wiþ; I bere þe writ riȝt here."
> "Is it enseled?" I seide; "may men see þe lettres?"
> "Nay," he seide, "I seke hym þat haþ þe seel to kepe,
> And þat is cros and cristendom and crist þeron to honge;
> And whan it is enseled þerwiþ I woot wel þe soþe
> That Luciferis lordshipe laste shal no lenger."
>
> (B.XVII.1–8)

The connection between Moses and Christ, between the Ten Commandments and the Redemption, which we have encountered so many times before in the poem, receives here its full and explicit statement. The Commandments and the seal of Christendom are together the pardon that Truth purchased for Piers. Man's good works united with the grace of the Redemption make man "a god by þe gospel, a grounde and o lofte" (B.I.90). It is as if the pardon scene were being played over again, but analyzed into its separate parts, into its two separate moments in sacred history. Thus the "maundement" of Moses contains as yet only the human term of the mystery of truth. It has still to receive the divine endorsement, but Moses, or Hope, knows that it will. The dreamer here plays the part of the doubting priest in the earlier scene:

> "Lat se þi lettres," quod I, "we myghte þe lawe knowe."
> He plukkede forþ a patente, a pece of an hard roche
> Wheron was writen two wordes on þis wise yglosed.
> *Dilige deum & proximum tuum,*
> This was the tixte, trewely; I took ful good yeme.
> The glose was gloriously writen wiþ a gilt penne:

In hijs duobus mandatis tota lex pendet & prophete.
"Is here alle þi lordes lawes?" quod I; "ye, leue me," he seide.
"Whoso wercheþ after þis writ, I wol vndertaken,
Shal neuere deuel hym dere ne deeþ in soule greue;
For, þou3 I seye it myself, I haue saued with þis charme
Of men and of wommen many score þousand."

(B.XVII.10–21)[8]

As in the speech of Lady Holy Church and the unassigned speech in Passus XI, love is the law that Truth "lered . . . Moyses for þe leueste þyng and moost lik to heuene" (B.I.151). And the promise of Moses to those who follow this law is a paraphrase of Piers's psalm: "*si ambulauero in medio vmbre mortis, non timebo mala; quoniam tu mecum es.*"

Until the "maundement" gets the seal of Christendom, though, it is inadequate, as we see when, in acting out Christ's parable, Abraham (Faith, or the Priest) and Moses (Hope, or the Levite) both fail to help the man fallen among thieves. The Samaritan who does help is Charity, and soon we shall see that he is Piers and Christ as well. As Redeemer he will set the seal to the "maundement" of Moses:

"Haue hem excused," quod he; "hir help may litel auaille.
May no medicyne vnder mone þe man to heele brynge,
Neiþer Feiþ ne fyn hope, so festred be hise woundes,
Wiþouten þe blood of a barn born of a mayde."

(B.XVII.93–96)

He anticipates his role as Redeemer in his discussion of the messages of Faith and Hope. The dreamer had thought that the message of Faith, the doctrine of the Trinity, and that of Hope, the law of love, somehow competed with one another. He asked them rather querulously which he should follow: "It is lighter to lewed men o lesson to knowe / Than for to techen hem two, and to hard to lerne þe leeste!" (B.XVII.42–43). In response to the same question, the Samaritan says both teachings are to be accepted, thus leading us toward that synthesis of supernatural faith and natural morality which he will personify as Christ. He then gives a long, rather tedious exposition of the Trinity, comparing it first to a human hand and then to a burning

---

8. The Latin texts are Matt. 22:37–40.

torch. In the second case he transfers his metaphor to man, making man's moral acts an imitation of the Trinity:

"And as wex and weke and warm fir togideres
Fostren forþ a flawmbe and a fair leye . . .
So dooþ þe Sire and þe sone and also *spiritus sanctus*
Fostren forþ amonges folk loue and bileue
That alle kynne cristene clenseþ of synnes.

. . . .

For euery manere good man may be likned
To a torche or a tapur to reuerence þe Trinite,
And whoso morþereþ a good man, me þynkeþ, by myn Inwit,
He fordooþ þe leuest light þat oure lord louyeþ.
                                        (B.XVII.209–14, 281–84)

This is another elaboration of the ambiguous "truth" of Lady Holy Church and another explanation of how the creature's search for God generates His image. Thus Abraham's vision of the Trinity and Moses' "maundement" explain each other and lead man to heaven where God teaches His angels "þoruȝ þe Trinitee þe treuþe to knowe" (B.I.109).

An optical metaphor may help here to explain the relation of this stage of the poem's development to the pardon scene. If, when looking into a stereoscope, one pulls the plate slightly away from the right focal length, the picture, which was clear and had solidity and depth, becomes two pictures which lack depth and overlap so as to hinder each other's clarity. When Piers received the pardon, the dreamer's "picture" came to a focus in the coincidence of divine and human spheres of action, of Grace and Nature. Each explained the other. Each gave the other a clarity and depth that neither possessed alone. The ordinary goodness of man gained a supernatural dimension, and truth was transparent to Truth. The carping priest upset the focus and separated the divine and human into flat, mutually distorting pictures. So the dreamer was sent off on his search for the "Do-well" which in itself constitutes the best pardon because it denotes the cooperation of human good works with the divine graces won in the Redemption. As he approaches his goal, there is a sense of converging, quickening movement. His last three instructors move rapidly down a straight road to Jerusalem. Their multiple identities exemplify Langland's clearest use of biblical typology and show the merging of different levels of meaning which the dreamer had been trying so hard to reconcile. Historical time refracts in them as they approach its intersection with eternity in the Redemption. This is extreme in the case of the Samaritan who outdistances the rest on his "Capul þat highte *caro*" (B.XVII.110), and becomes at once Samaritan, Charity, Piers, and Christ. One could say, then, that the whole poem from Passus VIII to Passus XVII is an attempt to put the pardon scene back together again; or, to put it in terms that lead us to our second problem, to bring Piers the Plowman back into the world.

The character Piers the Plowman is introduced with so little commentary, and the recognition of his authority, if not of its extent, is so immediate, that one is almost compelled, as Frank says, to seek him in "some context outside the poem that made him more easily intelligible to fourteenth-century readers than he is today."[9] But the search for sources has been inconclusive and will probably never account for this dearest child of Langland's imagination.

To discover who he is, we should first ask how and where one finds him. When he first appears, Reason and Repentance have just given sermons of such power that all the Seven Deadly Sins have been moved to contrition. The very presence in the public world of the personified virtues indicates the coalescence of society into an ideal form which makes it an apt subject of grace. But the source of grace is elsewhere, as Repentance acknowledges in his prayer:

> "I shal biseche for alle synfulle oure Saueour of grace
> To amenden vs of oure mysdedes: do mercy to vs alle,
> God, þat of þi goodnesse gonne þe world make,
> And of nauȝt madest auȝt and man moost lik to þiselue,
> And siþen suffredest hym to synne, a siknesse to vs alle,
> And for þe beste as I bileue whateuere þe book telleþ:
> *O felix culpa, o necessarium peccatum Ade &c.*
> For þoruȝ þat synne þi sone sent was to erþe
> And bicam man of a maide mankynde to saue,
> And madest þiself wiþ þi sone vs synfulle yliche:
> *Faciamus hominem ad ymaginem et similitudinem nostram;*
> *Et alibi, Qui manet in caritate in deo manet & deus in eo.*

9. Frank, *Salvation*, p. 14.

And siþþe wiþ þi selue sone in oure sute deidest
On good fryday for mannes sake at ful tyme of þe daye;
· · · · · · · · · ·

Aboute mydday, whan moost liȝt is and meel tyme of Seintes,
Feddest wiþ þi fresshe blood oure forefadres in derknesse:
Populus qui ambulabat in tenebris vidit lucem magnam.
The liȝt þat lepe out of þee, Lucifer it blente
And blewe alle þi blessed into þe blisse of Paradys.
· · · · · · · · · ·

And by so muche it semeþ þe sikerer we mowe
Bidde and biseche, if it be þi wille,
That art oure fader and oure broþer, be merciable to vs,
And haue ruþe on þise Ribaudes þat repenten hem soore
That euere þei wraþed þee in þis world in word, þouȝt or dedes."
(B.V.478–88, 492–95, 501–5)[10]

This prayer is a detailed anticipation of Passus XVIII, and there can
be no doubt that Langland so intended it, because the passage does
not appear in the A-text, which stops so far short of Passus XVIII.
The people in this earlier scene are ready to receive the grace of the
Redemption because their diverse wills are merged all into one:

A þousand of men þo þrungen togideres,
Cride vpward to Crist and to his clene moder
To haue grace to go to truþe, God leue þat þei moten.
(B.V.510–12)

But they cannot make the journey alone. Without a guide, they
"blustreden forþ as beestes ouer baches and hilles" (B.V.514). After
they have found a professional pilgrim unqualified, a guide suddenly
emerges from their midst:

"Peter!" quod a Plowman, and putte forþ his hed:
"I knowe hym as kyndely as clerc doþ hise bokes.
Conscience and kynde wit kenned me to his place

10. The Latin texts are from the canticle "Exultet" sung on Holy Saturday,
as given in the Sarum Missal (see *Parallel Texts* 2:98); Gen. 1:26; 1 John
4:16; and Isa. 9:2. On the tradition behind lines 494–95 see Thomas D. Hill,
"The Light that Blew the Saints to Heaven: B, V, 495–503," *Review of English
Studies* 24 (1973):444–49.

And diden me suren hym siþþen to seruen hym for euere,
Boþe sowe and sette while I swynke myȝte.

. . . .

I wol wisse yow wel riȝt to his place."

(B.V.537–41, 555)

He appears with the suddenness of a spark that leaps from one elec-
tric terminal to another, ready to take these people from their hard-
won, repentant truth to the Truth who is heaven's King.

For a gloss on this scene, we might recall briefly that passage in the
C-text which we discussed at length in chapter 3, the complicated
grammatical analogy by which Conscience explained the difference
between meed and mercede. According to this analogy, the true man
in this world is like an adjective who "Seketh and seweth his sustantif
sauacioun" and, by so doing, "acordeth with crist in kynde, *verbum
caro factum est*" (C.IV.355, 358). A society of true men is one governed by love, law, and leute, and in this social context there is a
shift in the grammatical relation of "kind": "alle maner men,
wymmen, and childrene / Sholde confourme hem to o kynde, on holy
kyrke to bileue" (C.IV.399–400). Where man agreed individually
with Christ in kind, he now agrees socially with his fellow men in
kind. He does this, though, for the sake of the love of Christ who

> coueytede oure kynde and be kald in oure name
> *Deus homo*
> And nyme hym in to oure noumbre now and euere more
> *Qui in caritate manet in deo manet et deus in eo.*
> Thus is man and mankynde in maner of a sustantyf
> As *hic et hec homo* askyng an adiectyf
> Of thre trewe termisones *trinitas vnus deus*
> *Nominatiuo pater et filius et spiritus sanctus.*

(C.IV.404–9)

Once again the relation of kind is between Christ and man, but, having passed through its social projection where it was between men,
the terms of its accord are reversed. Now man is the substantive, and
God is the adjective.

Something like this happens in the sudden appearance of Piers the
Plowman. The people, by their united cry "vpward to Crist," show
their accordance in kind. When Repentance mentions our likeness to

God, he illustrates it with the verse from Saint John's epistle: "*qui manet in caritate, in deo manet, et deus in eo.*" The C-text takes this verse away from Repentance and inserts it in Conscience's speech to illustrate how God seeks his substantive in the man of social love. Piers is the *homo* of *Deus homo*, and he emerges from the crowd as a symbol of their coalescence "to o kynde" through love. He is the substantive sought by God, and our search for him is actually God's search for us.[11]

This explains why he can propose the Ten Commandments to the people as the way to their supernatural goal. For their performance of natural good works is modified by the grace of the Incarnation just as a substantive is modified by an adjective. In a real sense, then, the work on Piers's half-acre *is* the pilgrimage of Truth and not merely a necessary delay before its beginning.[12] His role as the substantive of *Deus homo* also explains his role in setting up an ideal society on the half-acre. Piers is both a cause and a symptom of that ideal social order which agrees "in Kynde" and shadows forth the divine Idea. The pardon from Truth consecrates his work, but the priest's mockery destroys it. The priest, as a representative of the Church, the *corpus mysticum* of Christ, should recognize the worth of the pardon, that is, he should recognize and preach the value of good works in the context of grace. The viability of Piers's holy society depends on such perception in its officials. Failing this, the *corpus mysticum* loses its soul. Society becomes incoherent and blurs the divine Idea. Piers Plowman goes into hiding. One could even say with Wells, Chambers, and others, that he retires to the contemplative life, but this is not intended simply as the praise of a higher calling than life in the world. Rather, it is an indictment of a society that makes God invisible except to those who leave it, a society that rejects the corporate salvation offered by the Incarnation.

Piers is absent in the *Vita-de-Dowel* (at least in the B-text), because that section records the dreamer's attempts to regain internally

11. Cf. Nevill Coghill, "The Character of Piers Plowman Considered from the B-Text," *Medium Aevum* 2 (1933):119: ". . . but it would be truer to say . . . that Jesus *lives* Piers (for Piers is a way of Life) than that Jesus *is* Piers or that Piers *is* Jesus." Although the main argument of this article follows a rigid version of Wells's "Three Lives" theory, it remains one of the best discussions of the identity of Piers. See also Sister Mary Clemente Davlin, O.P., "*Petrus id est Christus*: Piers the Plowman as 'the Whole Christ,' " *Chaucer Review* 16 (1971–72):280–92.

12. A point made, in different terms, by John Burrow, "The Action of Langland's Second Vision," *Essays in Criticism* 15 (1965):254–59.

the coherence he saw briefly in society when Piers received the pardon. Piers is mentioned frequently, though—and in C he actually
appears[13]—in the discussion between the gluttonous Friar, Conscience, Clergy, and Patience on the definitions of Do-well, Do-bet,
and Do-best. The scene follows the dialogue with Imaginatif which
reconciled the dreamer to the difficulties of the intellectual life. Clergy
now admits the inadequacy of his forces to give an adequate definition
of the three "Do's," thus symbolizing the dreamer's fitness to move
beyond learning into the area of mystery:

> "For oon Piers þe Plowman haþ impugned vs alle,
> And set alle sciences at a sop saue loue one;
> And no text ne takeþ to mayntene his cause
> But *Dilige deum* and *Domine quis habitabit*;
> And demeþ that dowel and dobet arn two Infinites,
> Whiche Infinites wiþ a feiþ fynden out dobest,
> Which shal saue mannes soule; þus seiþ Piers þe Plowman."
>
> (B.XIII.124–30)

This seems the most vague of the many definitions of Do-well, Do-bet,
and Do-best, and it could include them all. In fact, Piers's formula
sounds like a description of the procession of the Trinity,[14] and, as
such, it recalls what the exercise of love makes of a man in a world
where the appearance of Piers is a possibility, in a universe informed
by grace. The man who does well in this most perfect sense is like a
"sustantyf" seeking an "adiectyf / Of thre trewe termisones *trinitas*

13. This change is a corollary of the C-text's revision of the second inner
dream. There the powers of the Trinity are wielded by *Liberum-Arbitrium*
rather than by Piers, as in B. The effect of both changes is to bring the Trinity
into contact with the human will without the intercession of Piers. He is no
longer given credit for a description of the three Do's in terms suggestive of
the Trinity in this earlier scene; and, later, he has no share in the internal
drama by which the Trinity helps man's will turn to God.

14. It may also be another instance of grammatical metaphor, since "infinite" can also describe a verb form (the infinitive) or an interrogative pronoun, both of which "seek" the specification of inflection or of response. See
Anne Middleton, "Two Infinites: Grammatical Metaphor in *Piers Plowman*,"
ELH 39 (1972):169–88. Parts of her argument seem to me overingenious,
based too much on linkages of wordplay found not in Langland but in his
putative sources among the grammarians. Also, she consistently speaks of the
definition as Clergy's when Clergy presents it as Piers's and does not even claim
to understand it clearly. The latter portion of her essay (181ff.) develops some
cogent generalizations on the role of grammatical metaphor in Langland's
allegory. The two Latin texts in this passage are Matt. 22:37, 39, and Ps. 15:1.

vnus deus." When we next see Piers he will be wielding the powers of the Trinity to aid man's will in its pursuit of Do-well.

When the dreamer meets Anima, in whom all the internal faculties converge and reveal themselves in action, the conversation gradually centers on Piers, and shows more clearly than elsewhere in the poem the influence of Saint Bernard and his followers. Will first asks what charity is:

> "a childissh þyng," he seide:
>
> .   .   .   .
>
> "Wiþouten fauntelte or folie a fre liberal wille."
>
> (B.XV.149–50)

This recalls Piers's promise in his first appearance that obedience to the Ten Commandments would win us the vision of Truth in our own hearts, "In a cheyne of charite as þow a child were, / To suffren hym and segge noȝt ayein þi sires wille" (B.V.607–8).[15] It also seems to satisfy Will's claims for the holy simplicity which pierces "wiþ a Paternoster þe paleys of heuene" (B.X.468). But we now know that we truly attain such simplicity by a transcendence of "Clergy," not a rejection of him.

Will complains that he never has seen charity in the world, and then, without any explicit transition, asks about Christ:

> Clerkes kenne me þat crist is in alle places
> Ac I seiȝ hym neuere sooþly but as myself in a Mirour:
> *Hic in enigmate, tunc facie ad faciem.*
>
> (B.XV.161–62)

Will here makes the same use of 1 Corinthians 13:12 as most of the mystics do, and he may also have had in mind a passage from the Epistle General of James. There we are told that a man who has faith without works, who is a hearer and not a doer, is like a man "considering his natural face in a mirror: for he considered himself, and went away, and immediately forgot what he was like." The man who "looks into the perfect law of liberty and perseveres becomes not a forgetful hearer but a doer of works: this man will be blessed in his works."[16] As I suggested in connection with the pardon, James's

15. Both these passages make their first appearance in B.
16. James 1:23–25. I am indebted to Professor Donaldson for calling this passage to my attention.

epistle is full of reflections on the relationship of faith and works which seem very close to the thought of Langland. It seems particularly close here where the dreamer's halting search for Charity, the basis of all good works, is marked by fleeting glimpses in a mirror of himself or of Christ. The context of the whole poem gives these glimpses a social meaning as well. For if charity were to be found in society, if men agreed in kind through love, law, and leute, then Christ would be seen "in alle places." Man would see in society his own reflected image as "in a Mirour," and society would be transformed by grace into one kind with Christ. As it is, the image of man and hence of God can come to a steady focus only subjectively, in the soul. This coming to a focus is heralded internally, as externally, by the figure of Piers:

> "By crist! I wolde I knewe hym," quod I, "no creature leuere."
> "Wiþouten help of Piers Plowman," quod he, "his persone sestow
>   neuere."
> "Wheiþer clerkes knowen hym," quod I, "þat kepen holi kirke?"
> "Clerkes haue no knowyng," quod he, "but by werkes and
>   wordes.
> Ac Piers þe Plowman parceyueþ moore depper
> What is þe wille and wherfore þat many wight suffreþ:
> *Et vidit deus cogitaciones eorum.*"
>
>   (B.XV.195–200)[17]

Here, as Skeat notes, "*Piers the Plowman* is completely identified with *Jesus Christ*."[18] Anima follows up with a more explicit statement:

> "Therfore by colour ne by clergie knowe shaltow hym neuere,
> Neiþer þoruჳ wordes ne werkes, but þoruჳ wil oone,
> And þat knoweþ no clerk ne creature on erþe
> But Piers þe Plowman, *Petrus id est christus.*"
>
>   (B.XV.209–12)

If some critics boggle at this identification, so indeed did Langland. In the C-text, the line disappears, the difficulty of finding charity is lessened somewhat, and the extended role of *Liberum-Arbitrium* brings the whole line of argument closer to an irreproachable source

---

17. The Latin refers either to Matt. 9:4 or to Luke 11:17.
18. *Parallel Texts*, 2:221.

in Bernardine mysticism.[19] That Langland was so concerned about covering his bets shows that he was risking a good deal in the B-text. When he said "Petrus id est christus," he meant just that. He does not really change his ideas in the C-text, but he gives them a more diffuse expression in *Liberum-Arbitrium* and in Conscience's grammatical analysis of *Deus homo*. Langland's sense of the continuity of the human and the divine after the Incarnation remains just as strong—and potentially heretical—in C as it was in B. But it becomes a more difficult target than when embodied in one symbolic plowman.

The appearance of Piers in the inner dream, tending the Tree of Charity "Amyddes mannes body," gives the poem as a whole a certain symmetry. The approach in the outer, social world to the coherence that makes men agree with one another and with Christ in kind was marked by the appearance of Piers with his directions for finding Truth. The approach to inner, intellectual and spiritual coherence is likewise attended by Piers in the role of teacher. If both coherences could be maintained, if the inner and outer worlds reflected each other and equally revealed the divine Idea, then Piers would be continually present. He is at once the intersection of subjective and objective and of the divine and human realms. It is a symptom of the dissociation of these realms that he shows up only momentarily, now in one, now in another.

But his presence in the inner dream could seem redundant. Donaldson raises "the objection that if Piers is to be understood as man in the vision of the tree, then man is thrice represented—once in Piers, once in the fruit of the tree, and once by Liberum Arbitrium, man's free will."[20] As Donaldson demonstrates, the C-text clarified the scene by substituting *Liberum-Arbitrium*, man's free will, for Piers. We have examined the significance of that change in some detail in chapter 2. It remains to be seen what sacrifices Langland made for the sake of logical clarity and doctrinal safety, and whether some sense can be made of Piers's role in B.

The inner dream presents us with a sort of inverse of the typological procedure which makes several meanings converge in the single figures of Abraham, Moses, and the Samaritan. Here, inside man, the

---

19. Principally because the whole commentary is spoken by *Liberum-Arbitrium* instead of Anima, and he, not Piers, undergoes the deification in the first Passus of Dobet. The force and application of the Latin text, "*Et vidit deus cogitationes eorum*," is also altered in C.XVII.337–39.

20. *C-Text.* p. 187.

meanings diverge into several separate figures. One can draw a partial parallel between the several figures "Amyddes mannes body" and the several meanings of the most polysemous of Will's subsequent instructors, the Samaritan. In both groups, one eventually finds Piers, Charity (which is a "fre liberal wille" and so connected with *Liberum-Arbitrium* as well as the Tree), and Christ. One must admit, however, that the different meanings are handled more deftly in the figure of the Samaritan.

Liberum-Arbitrium, as we saw in chapter 2, is, by one account, the faculty which bears the image of God. As described by Piers it works so much in unison with the Holy Spirit as to be almost indistinguishable from it. It is the direct recipient within man of grace. But the granting of grace has complications both individually and historically. Its presence in each man implies both the Fall and the Redemption. Hence the mystery of its operations requires three different figures for its adequate poetic representation, even though this may seem redundant. We are threatened by the Devil because our human nature is that of Adam who fell and brought down with him "Abraham and Ysaye þe prophete, / Sampson and Samuel and Seint Iohan þe Baptist" (B.XVI.81–82) and all the fruit of Piers's tree. We can resist because we bear God's image in our free will (*Liberum-Arbitrium*); but we can defeat the Devil only by help of the graces of the Incarnation by which our human nature (Piers) was assumed and redeemed by the Son of God:

> And Piers for pure tene þat a pil he lauȝte;
> He hitte after hym, happe how it myȝte,
> *Filius* by þe fader wille and frenesse of *spiritus sancti*.
>
> (B.XVI.86–88)

So there is a kind of logic to the scene as it appears in B, the kind of logic proper to dreams and visionary poetry. In fact, the streamlining in C is open to some challenges in terms of the more prosaic logic it seems to have sought. To make *Liberum-Arbitrium* the recipient of Christ's divine nature is to admit too much of what is divine and too little of what is human. *Liberum-Arbitrium* is the image of the entire Trinity, whereas Christ is only the second Person of the Trinity. Christ took on the entire human nature, whereas *Liberum-Arbitrium* is only one faculty of human nature. Finally, in the C-text, the reader may be somewhat nonplussed to see in the Christ of Passus XXI "On was

semblable to the Samaritan and somdel to Peers Plouhman" (C.XXI.
8). We have been prepared for this line in B (XVIII.10) by the
deification of Piers in the inner dream.

The C-text usually tries to tame the exuberance that tempts B to
the frontiers of logic and beyond, but in one notable exception to this
rule, Conscience's grammatical analogy, the exuberance takes revenge
on this repression and shows that the author, for all his good intentions, is still William Langland. The passage in C can, I think, cast
some light backward on the inner dream in B. The Tree of Charity
in one of its aspects is an image of society as a whole. As the fruits
of one tree, the members of society, whether married, widows, or
virgins, agree in "o kynde," to borrow the C-text's term. This is confirmed by the superimposed image of the patriarchs and prophets who
were the prime types of human righteousness awaiting grace. Before
this society made one through love stands Piers the Plowman, just as
he stood forth when "a þousand of men . . . Cride vpward to Crist."
He stands before it as its type, symbolizing its readiness for the gift
of grace. As in the earlier social setting, he is the *homo* of *Deus
homo*, the "sustantyf . . . askyng an adiectyf / Of thre trewe termisones *trinitas vnus deus*," and receiving it in the "piles" which prop
up the Tree of Charity. The ideal society, here as elsewhere, finds its
image in the human heart. At this point we are approaching the source
of that image in the Redemption, beyond which lies the tragic effort
to project it into the world once again.

There is a difficult passage near the beginning of the story of the
Redemption that breaks in when Piers takes up the second prop
against the devil. The Holy Spirit tells Mary

> That oon Iesus a Iustices sone moste Iouke in hir chambre.
>
> . . . .
>
> And in þe wombe of þat wenche was he fourty woukes
> Til he weex a faunt þoruȝ hir flessh and of fightyng kouþe
> To haue yfouȝte wiþ þe fend er ful tyme come.
> And Piers þe Plowman parceyued plener tyme
> And lered hym lechecraft his lif for to saue
> That, þouȝ he were wounded with his enemy, to warisshen hym-
>   selue;
> And dide hym assaie his surgenrie on hem þat sike were
> Til he was parfit praktisour if any peril fille.
> And souȝte oute þe sike and saluede blynde and crokede,

And commune wommen conuertede and clensed of synne,
And sike and synfulle boþe so to goode turnede:
Non est sanis opus medicus set infirmis.

(B.XVI.92, 100–110)

Donaldson has confessed bewilderment at the odd relationship here of Piers to Christ, noting that "The point is a doctrinal one, with its roots heaven knows where."[21] R. E. Kaske has sought its source in commentaries on the Gospels which make the Holy Spirit the instructor of Christ. This is a good deal easier in the C-text, where *Liberum-Arbitrium*, not Piers, is Christ's teacher. Kaske appeals to the association between this personified faculty and the Holy Ghost, demonstrated by Donaldson in his discussion of the inner dream.[22] His point may be well taken, but he begs the question when he carries this reading back into the B-text, thus creating the false problem of how to hold on both to the Holy Ghost and to Piers's "fundamental role in the poem as man."[23] He solves the problem by positing a "complex relationship between Piers and John the Baptist," by which Piers's role would stand for that of John in the inauguration of the public life of Christ. "In terms of the surface Gospel narrative, John's teaching Christ leechcraft might be read as an allegorizing of his visible human role as precursor of Christ (much emphasized in the commentaries), living a similarly blameless life, preparing Christ's way by preaching a similar gospel, and at Christ's baptism serving as minister of the Holy Ghost. The more important allegorical significance of John's teaching Christ, however, would depend on the common spiritual interpretation of John as God's grace, here obviously suggesting the grace of the Holy Ghost by which Christ is taught after His baptism—and, incidentally, providing an understandable basis for the substitution of *Liberum-Arbitrium* (the Holy Ghost) in the C-Text."[24] One could as easily say that the substitution provides "an understandable basis" for Kaske's interpretation of the C-text; but it has already served as a basis for his interpretation of the B-text's original. If Kaske's interpretation of C is correct—and it may well be—then there is a fundamental change from the meaning of the

21. Ibid., p. 184.
22. R. E. Kaske, "Patristic Exegesis: The Defense," in Dorothy Bethurum, ed., *Critical Approaches to Medieval Literature* (New York: Columbia University Press, 1960), p. 44. Cf., Donaldson, *C-Text*, pp. 191–92.
23. Ibid., p. 47.
24. Ibid., pp. 47–48.

passage in B.[25] There Piers is simply the human nature of Christ, and his lessons in leechcraft must be explained in terms of that role.

Kaske points out, correctly, that the first lines of the passage are a figurative paraphrase of Luke 2:40: "And the boy grew and was strengthened, full of wisdom: and the grace of God was in him."[26] Luke 2:52 might do as well: "And Jesus advanced in wisdom and age and grace [or favor] before God and men." These verses involve us in many of the same difficulties as we find in Piers's role as Christ's teacher. In what sense could Christ, the Son of God, be said to grow in strength or wisdom, since, as God, he was the perfection of both? Commentators generally answered the question by making a distinction between the divine and human natures and insisting that with his other, divine sorts of knowledge Christ also possessed human knowledge, which must be acquired.[27] This might seem to imply a defect in the Godhead, but the Incarnate Christ possessed perfect manhood as well and so "nothing that God planted in our nature was wanting to the human nature assumed by the Word of God."[28] Saint Thomas applies this to Luke 2:52: "The infused knowledge as well as the beatific knowledge of Christ's soul were the effects of an agent of infinite power, Who can produce His whole effect at once. And so in neither knowledge did Christ advance, but rather had each perfectly from the start. But acquired knowledge is caused by the active intellect, which does not produce its whole effect at once, but in stages. And thus according to this knowledge Christ did not know everything at once, but little by little and after a certain time, that is to say, when he came of age. This is clear from what the Evangelist says, that he advanced in knowledge and age together."[29] If Christ, because of His human nature, could *acquire* knowledge, we could say, poetically, that He was *taught* by His human nature. So Piers, Christ's perfect human nature,

---

25. Erzgräber (*William Langlands Piers Plowman*, pp. 176, 181–82) proposes another explanation of *Liberum-Arbitrium's* instructions to Christ which is simpler and perhaps for that reason preferable. He suggests that the Incarnation is the expression of that "*Libera-Voluntas-Dei*" that "lauhte the myddel shoriere" (C.XIX.119) and that *Liberum-Arbitrium* in C.XIX.138 is synonymous with this. This, like Kaske's reading, is a significant change from B.

26. "Patristic Exegesis," p. 44.

27. See Saint Thomas Aquinas, *Catena Aurea: Commentary on the Four Gospels Collected out of the Works of the Fathers*, III, part 1 (Oxford, 1843), p. 95, for comments of Bede and Cyril.

28. Saint Thomas, *Summa Theologiae* 3a.9.4, *respondeo*.

29. Ibid. 3a.12.2, *ad* 1. See, further, "Jésus-Christ," in *Dict. de Théol. Cath.*, 8:1259–60; and "Science de Jésus-Christ," ibid., 14.1627–65, esp. 1630, 1635–38, 1657–59.

was Christ's teacher, giving his lesson only as he "parceyued plener tyme."

But why "lechecraft"? In answering this we might first note the Latin tag line which, perhaps significantly, disappears from the C-text. It approximates a saying of Christ: "Those who are whole do not need a physician, but those who are sick."[30] Rabanus Maurus comments that "He calls himself a physician, because by a wonderful kind of medicine He was wounded for our iniquities that He might heal the wound of our sin."[31] This means, or it might have meant to Langland, that Christ, by taking on a human nature capable of suffering, was learning how to cure His suffering, fallen human creatures. The idea of Christ's learning from His human nature is developed along similar lines by Saint Bernard. He begins by saying that we must learn to share the sorrows of our fellow men in order to help them. In this we follow "the example of our Savior Who wished His passion, that He might know compassion, His misery that He might know commiseration, so that just as it is written of Him, 'He learned obedience by the things He suffered' (Hebrews 5.8), so He learned mercy as well. Not that He did not know how to be merciful before, Whose mercy is from eternity to eternity, but that what He knew from eternity by His Nature He learned in time by experience."[32] I think that this association of ideas lies behind the leechcraft taught Christ by Piers. In order to be a physician to men, physically and spiritually, Christ had to go to the school of His human nature. He had to learn man's frailties and sufferings as men do, bit by bit, until at "plener tyme" He could do battle for them. If we did not have Bernard's' commentary, we might appeal to that of Peace, the lady who came out of the south to witness the Harrowing of Hell:

> "So god þat bigan al of his goode wille
> Bicam man of a mayde mankynde to saue
> And suffrede to be sold to se þe sorwe of deying,
> The which vnknytteþ alle care and comsynge is of reste.

. . . .

30. See Matt. 9:12, Mark 2:17, and Luke 5:31, none of which is in just these words.

31. A comment on Matt. 9:12 collected in Saint Thomas, *Catena Aurea*, I, part 1 (Oxford, 1841), p. 339.

32. Saint Bernard, *Tractatus de gradibus humilitatis et superbiae* 3.6, in *PL* 182:944D–945A. Cf. Gilson, *The Mystical Theology of Saint Bernard*, pp. 75–78; Saint Thomas, *Summa Theologiae* 3.15; and "Jésus-Christ," in *Dict. de Théol. Cath.*, 8:1327–32.

Forþi god, of his goodnesse, þe firste gome Adam,
Sette hym in solace and in souereyn murþe,
And siþþe he suffred hym synne sorwe to feele,
To wite what wele was, kyndeliche to knowe it.
And after god Auntrede hymself and took Adames kynde
To se what he haþ suffred in þre sondry places,
Boþe in heuene and in erþe, and now til helle he þenkeþ
To wite what alle wo is þat woot of alle ioye.

(B.XVIII.212–15, 218–25)

When Christ has learned the last lesson that Piers can teach Him, then Piers and mankind will be saved. This is the paradox of the Incarnation and of Langland's plowman. Here the divine and human meet with such an intimacy and a union of wills that it seems almost as though they gain equally from the encounter.

Piers's role as teacher suggests a point we made earlier, that if the dreamer's search has been for the image of God in himself and in the world, we can almost say that in the figure of Piers we have evidence of God's search for the image of man. Lady Holy Church had said that God's love was almost compelled to alloy itself with earth, and that it gained in agility and strength from the Incarnation:

"And whan it hadde of þis fold flessh and blood taken
Was neuere leef vpon lynde lighter þerafter,
And portatif and persaunt as þe point of a nedle
That myȝte noon Armure it lette ne none heiȝe walles."

(B.I.155–58)

When the Samaritan—who is also Charity and Christ—outdistances his companions and outdares the Devil, he gives the credit to his "Capul þat highte *caro*—of mankynde I toke it" (B.XVII.110; dropped by C). When Christ jousted with the Devil, he had to look to man for his armor:

"This Iesus of his gentries wol Iuste in Piers armes,
In his helm and in his haubergeon, *humana natura*;
That crist be noȝt yknowe here for *consummatus deus*
In Piers paltok þe Plowman þis prikiere shal ryde,
For no dynt shal hym dere as *in deitate patris*."

(B.XVIII.22–26)

This is an intensely paradoxical passage, for in this special kind of joust, where Christ's death will be His victory, human vulnerability must act as a shield to protect divine invulnerability. Small wonder, then, that the Redemption turns out to be an elaborate joke on the Devil whose last defense is a frantic effort to keep Christ alive (B. XVIII.300–306). Here, as elsewhere, God needs man for the full expression of His love. This sort of reversal of dependency suggests the divine *hubris* of Romantic poets (such as Blake and Shelley, the study of whom involves us in many of the same kinds of difficulty as the study of Langland). In fact, for a precise description of Langland's elusive plowman one could hardly do better than these lines of a great Christian Romantic, Gerard Manley Hopkins:

> Í say móre: the just man justices;
> Keéps gráce: thát keep all his goings graces;
> Acts in God's eye what in God's eye he is—
> Chríst—for Christ plays in ten thousand places,
> Lovely in limbs, and lovely in eyes not his
> To the Father through the features of men's faces.[33]

The mystery exists precisely in these two dependencies which intersect in Piers-Christ, through whom man looks to God for the amplification of his finite good works and God looks to man for the reflected image of His own beauty.

33. Sonnet: "As kingfishers catch fire, dragonflies draw flame," in *Poems*, ed. Robert Bridges, rev. W. H. Gardner (New York and London: Oxford University Press, 1948), p. 95.

6. The Essential Poem at the Centre
of Things

W HAT ARE WE to make, finally, of a poem of such shape and such scope? We easily perceive its essential unity, but how do we articulate that perception? Generic classification must prove a blind alley for a poem so intractably *sui generis*. One can call *Piers Plowman* a dream vision, a "complaint," a *consolatio*, a social satire, or any number of other things. All of these titles would fit tolerably well, but they would be appreciably less informative than the characterization of Words-worth's *Prelude* as a *Bildungsroman*. What escapes such classification in the case of *Piers Plowman* is the voice of the poet Langland as he tries single-handedly to pull the diverse and contradictory world he sees about him into a coherent shape that will show him his face "as . . . in a Mirour" and the God Whose image he is. The ambitiousness of such an undertaking and the clear awareness of just what it entails seem to have been enough to provide Langland with a life's work and to burst the bounds of any received generic structure.

As I suggested at the end of my last chapter, the judgments we must make of Langland are in some respects similar to those we must make of some of the greater Romantic poets. His poem seems to me to be "organic" in their sense of the term.[1] In a manner that has recently been described as "non-medieval," his structures and his metaphors

1. See M. H. Abrams, *The Mirror and the Lamp* (New York: Oxford University Press, 1953), pp. 57–59, 218–25, on the "organic" in Romantic thought. See also Robert M. Jordan, *Chaucer and the Shape of Creation* (Cambridge: Harvard University Press, 1967), pp. 3–9, and passim, for a characterization of medieval art in general and Chaucer's art in particular as "inorganic."

constantly break down before his growing, evolving vision of a truth they can no longer embody.[2] So the poem follows no straight path. Instead, its serpentine movement through an expanding network of ideas and images and phrases reaches ever wider to include ever more of God's creation in a field of potential grace and light. At the same time, the difference between the potential and the reality of the world he would save is never lost on Langland, and can excite him at any point to invective satire. In the end, this disenchanted awareness is definitive, as it must be in a poem which refuses to falsify the world it would redeem.

In Wordsworth's poetry, the recognition of something related to him in Nature, some structural similarity to the workings of his own mind, seems to put him in touch with an absolute higher than himself or Nature, the two parties to the encounter. In Langland the encounter is principally in the social or the intellectual realm, but it involves a similar intimation of a transcendent absolute, symbolized by Piers himself, who is the human nature assumed by God. What "Imagination . . . the Power so called / Through sad incompetence of human speech"[3] does for one poet, grace and the Redemption do for the other, as both look out upon a world transformed by their vision of it. In both poets the presence of this power must be realized again and again in moments of vision whose transitoriness defines the tragic human condition.

I took the title of this final chapter from Wallace Stevens, who is, among other things, an heir of Wordsworth in his celebration of those moments of radiant order when the imagination and reality intersect. He is also an atheist and so might seem out of place in a study of so profoundly Christian a poet as Langland. But poetry constitutes its own catholic church, and poems are usually the best expositors of other poems. The story of the Incarnation and Redemption is certainly not an ordering principle to Stevens, but its function as such for Langland could not be better described than in Stevens's words:

> The essential poem at the centre of things,
> The arias that spiritual fiddlings make,

2. See Rosemary Woolf, "Some Non-Medieval Qualities of *Piers Plowman*," *Essays in Criticism* 12 (1962):111–25; and John Burrow, "The Action of Langland's Second Vision," *Essays in Criticism* 15 (1965):247–68, which discusses "that peculiar movement of Langland's thought . . . a 'serpent-like' movement towards more inward statements" (p. 267) in B.VI and VII.

3. *The Prelude* (1850), 6:592–93.

Have gorged the cast-iron of our lives with good
And the cast-iron of our works.

For Langland, as for Stevens, "The roundness that pulls tight the final ring" is not a set, formulated answer to any of his questions. It is, instead,

A vis, a principle or, it may be,
The meditation of a principle,
Or else an inherent order active to be
Itself, a nature to its natives all
Beneficence, a repose, utmost repose,
The muscles of a magnet aptly felt,
A giant, on the horizon, glistening.

For both poets, the sense of coherence they seek in external reality is something that moves, something that lives, something finally that coalesces to a human shape. For one, it is the shape of a giant; for the other, that of a plowman. And when this shape appears in the light of common day,

　　　　　　　　the used-to earth and sky, and the tree
And cloud, the used-to tree and used-to cloud,
Lose the old uses that they made of them,
And they: these men, and earth and sky, inform
Each other by sharp informations, sharp,
Free knowledges, secreted until then.

And all men who throng together, crying with one voice their need to find this central man, fuse into a new being, a *corpus mysticum*:

That's it. The lover writes, the believer hears,
The poet mumbles and the painter sees,
Each one, his fated eccentricity,
As a part, but part, but tenacious particle,
Of the skeleton of the ether, the total
Of letters, prophecies, perceptions, clods
Of color, the giant of nothingness, each one
And the giant ever changing, living in change.[4]

4. "A Primitive Like an Orb," in *The Collected Poems of Wallace Stevens* (New York: Alfred A. Knopf, 1954), pp. 440–43.

In the last lines, of course, the poets part company. For Langland it was no "giant of nothingness" he sought; but the search for his plowman and for Christ who fought in his flesh was no less difficult for that, in an England where God, if not dead, seemed to have turned away from His creatures in angry silence.

What Langland searches for is the essential poem with the essential hero, and, after many fitful glimpses of his goal, he achieves it in Passus XVIII of the B-text. All readers of the poem must feel this confident sense of arrival in the scene before the gates of hell when Langland can finally speak through the mouth of Christ Himself:

> "For I þat am lord of lif, loue is my drynke,
> And for þat drynke today I deide vpon erþe.
> I fauʒt so me þursteþ ʒit for mannes soule sake;
> May no drynke me moiste, ne my þurst slake,
> Til þe vendage falle in þe vale of Iosaphat,
> That I drynke riʒt ripe Must, *Resureccio mortuorum.*
> And þanne shal I come as a kyng, crouned, wiþ Aungeles,
> And haue out of helle alle mennes soules.
> Fendes and fendekynes bifore me shul stande
> And be at my biddyng wherso best me likeþ.
> Ac to be merciable to man þanne my kynde it askeþ
> For we beþ breþeren of blood, ac noʒt in baptisme alle.
> Ac alle þat beþ myne hole breþeren, in blood and in baptisme,
> Shul noʒt be dampned to þe deeþ þat dureþ wiþouten ende
> . . . .
> And my mercy shal be shewed to manye of my haluebreþeren,
> For blood may suffre blood boþe hungry and acale
> Ac blood may noʒt se blood blede but hym rewe."
>
>   (B.XVIII.365–78, 393–95)

The speech is remarkable for its sheer rhetorical power, and for its continuity with other parts of the poem, particularly the early speeches of Piers in his concern for his "blody bretheren."[5] This continuity is Langland's surest ground of hope. He knows that at one point in history God spoke with a human voice, and that if men come together in love to give Him back His voice, He will speak once again.

5. Especially B.VI.201–11, which is echoed in B.XI.197–211.

Index

Abrams, M. H., 123n
Active Intellect, 12
Adam of Woodham, 80, 84
Alain de Lille, 63, 69–70, 89
Amassian, Margaret, 45n, 47n
Ambrose, Saint, 21n
Anselm, Saint, 20
Apocalyptic tradition, 2, 33, 34–35, 38, 54, 58
Aquinas, Thomas. *See* Thomas Aquinas, Saint
Aristotle, 14, 47n, 73, 77n
Auerbach, Erich, 101n
Augustine, Saint, 2, 12, 15, 17, 20n, 21n, 38, 40, 43–44, 60, 66–67, 74, 77n, 81, 104n

Bernard, Saint, 2, 24, 27, 76, 115, 120
Blake, William, 122
Bloomfield, Morton W., 2n, 28n, 33, 50n, 54n, 61–62, 71, 91
Boehner, Philotheus, O.F.M., 82n
Bonaventure, Saint, 13–14, 15, 18–19, 22, 23, 55n, 56, 63, 74, 77, 95, 96
Boniface VIII, Pope, 37
Bradwardine, Thomas, 74, 81, 90
Burrow, John, 111n, 124

Carruthers, Mary, 40n, 101n
Cassiodorus, Flavius Magnus Aurelius, 67

Ceffons, Pierre de, 81n
Chambers, R. W., 2n, 74n, 86n, 111
Charles I, king of England, 35n
Clergy (personified character), 67–68, 70, 71–73, 85, 86, 88, 96, 112
Cloud of Unknowing, The, 63, 82–83
Coghill, Nevill, 2n, 31, 32, 99, 111n
Cohn, Norman, 33n
Conscience (personified character): his grammatical metaphor for Meed and *mercede*, 42–53, 110–11, 112, 115, 117; mentioned, 32–33, 34, 41, 57, 58, 62, 96
Copleston, Frederick, 12n, 14, 74n, 77n, 78n
Courcelle, Pierre, 76n
Crompton, James, 82n
Cupidity, 40–41, 43–44
Curtius, Ernst Robert, 44n, 67

Dante Alighieri, 20–21, 36–37, 38, 44, 58, 60, 69, 71n, 74, 85, 87n, 92n, 96
Davlin, Mary Clement, O.P., 111n
Divine Illumination, 12–16, 70, 78
Donaldson, E. Talbot, 1n, 2n, 5n, 6n, 16n, 24, 27, 36n, 37n, 47n, 53n, 66, 87n, 88n, 113n, 115, 118
Dunning, T. P., 6n, 31, 32, 41, 96n
Duns Scotus, John, 12n, 77, 78

Eckhart, Meister, 83

Erzgräber, Willi, 11*n*, 68*n*, 77, 119*n*
Exemplarism, 17–22

Fourfold sense of Scripture, 1, 54–55, 96
Frank, R. W., 2*n*, 86, 100–101, 108
"Free Spirit," heresy of the, 83
Friars, 50, 82*n*, 84

Gilson, Etienne, 13*n*, 14, 27*n*, 78*n*, 120*n*
Glossa Ordinaria, 104*n*

Henry of Marcy, 55
Hill, Thomas D., 109*n*
Hilton, Walter, 1, 63
Holkot, Robert, 80, 84, 86
Hollander, Robert, 37*n*
Holy Church, Lady, speech of, 5–9, 23, 27, 28–29, 33, 39, 42, 46, 51, 56, 69, 97, 102, 103, 106, 121
Hopkins, Gerard Manley, 122
Hort, Greta, 6*n*, 11, 24–26
Howard, Donald, 60*n*
Hugh of Saint Victor, 12*n*, 17–19, 21–22, 63, 68, 90*n*, 95
Huppé, Bernard F., 2*n*

Image and likeness of God: man as, 2–3, 16–20, 23–24, 95; in Triune aspect, 2, 25–26, 95–96, 106–7
Imaginatif (personified character), 63, 65, 89, 91–97
Incarnation, transformation of human good works by, 10, 48–49, 57–58, 111, 112–13
Inwit, defined as active intellect, 11–12
Isidore of Seville, 96*n*

Jones, H. S. V., 91*n*
Jordan, Robert M., 122*n*
Julian of Norwich, 82

Kane, George, 4, 5*n*, 16*n*, 37*n*, 44*n*, 88*n*
Kantorowicz, Ernst, 35, 36*n*, 51*n*
Kaske, R. E., 37*n*, 71, 96*n*, 118–19
Kean, P. M., 8*n*, 47
Kirk, Elizabeth, 11*n*, 28*n*, 50*n*, 87*n*, 98*n*, 102*n*
Knowles, M. David, 78*n*, 81*n*, 82*n*

Lawlor, John, 9*n*, 43*n*, 102*n*
Leff, Gordon, 74*n*, 75*n*, 77*n*, 79, 80*n*, 81, 82*n*, 83
Leute: as term, 47–48, 50–53; as personification, 52, 84–85
Liberum-Arbitrium, 24–30, 33, 34, 113*n*, 114–17, 118
Lombard, Peter, 104*n*
Lubàc, Henri de, 55, 58, 60

Maisack, Helmut, 76*n*, 83*n*
Meed, Lady: Conscience's rejection of, 41–53, 64, 65; mentioned, 32–33
Meroney, Howard, 101
Middleton, Anne, 112*n*
Minstrels, imagery of, 22–23, 52–53
Mitchell, A. G., 41, 42*n*, 43*n*, 45*n*, 49*n*
Mysticism, influence of, 2, 6–7, 38–39, 82–84, 88–89

Oberman, Heiko Augustinus, 86*n*
Ockham, William of, 74, 78–80, 81, 83, 86, 88, 89

Pantin, W. A., 74*n*
Pelzer, A., 79*n*
Peter, Saint, 59
Piers the Plowman: as the human nature of Christ, 3, 57–58, 59, 106, 110–22, 126; his directions to Truth, 9–10, 29, 39, 98; and the Tree of Charity, 24–30, 34, 56–57, 97, 112*n*, 115–17; and the pardon, 98–108
Plato, 34, 39*n*
Plowden, Edmund, 35*n*

Quirk, Randolph, 11–12, 91*n*

Rabanus Maurus, 120
Reason (personified character), 32–34, 89–91
Robertson, D. W., 2*n*
Robson, J. A., 81*n*, 82*n*
Russell, G. H., 45*n*, 47*n*

Sadowsky, James, 45*n*, 47*n*
Salter, Elizabeth, 9
"Sawles Warde," 12*n*
Schweitzer, Edward G., 96*n*

Scripture (personified character), 70–
74, 81, 83, 85, 88
Shelley, Percy Bysshe, 122
Singleton, Charles S., 58*n*
Sir Orfeo, 27*n*
Skeat, Walter W., 5*n*, 7*n*, 11*n*, 16*n*,
17*n*, 26*n*, 87*n*, 88*n*, 114
Smith, Ben H., Jr., 8*n*, 26*n*, 29*n*, 96*n*
Socrates, 39
Stevens, Wallace, 124–26
Study (personified character), 42, 64,
65–66, 68–69, 70, 87, 94, 95

Theology (personified character), 41–
42, 68–69, 94

Thomas Aquinas, Saint, 12, 14–15, 21*n*,
23*n*, 36*n*, 47*n*, 65*n*, 77, 119, 120*n*
Trajan, emperor of Rome, 86, 87, 103

Vasta, Edward, 2*n*, 6*n*, 76*n*

Wells, Henry W., 2*n*, 111
Wit, speech of, 10–23, 29, 33, 64, 88
Wittig, Joseph S., 11*n*, 21*n*, 74*n*, 85*n*,
87*n*, 91*n*, 92
Woolf, Rosemary, 101*n*, 102*n*, 124*n*
Wordsworth, William, 54*n*, 123, 124

Yunck, John, 42*n*

Zeeman, Elizabeth. *See* Salter, Elizabeth